First Mom

THE WIT AND WISDOM *of* BARBARA BUSH

edited by

BILL ADLER

RuggedLand

PUBLISHED BY RUGGED LAND, LLC
276 CANAL STREET · NEW YORK · NY · 10013 · USA

RUGGED LAND AND COLOPHON ARE TRADEMARKS OF RUGGED LAND, LLC.

PUBLISHER'S CATALOGING-IN-PUBLICATION DATA

Bush, Barbara, 1925-
First mom : the wit and wisdom of Barbara Bush / edited by Bill Adler.
p. cm.
LCCN 2003116458
ISBN 1590710266
1. Bush, Barbara, 1925---Quotations.
2. Presidents' spouses--United States--Quotations.
I. Adler, Bill, 1929- II. Title.

E 883.B87B87 2004   973.928'092
QBI33-1744

ALL INTERIOR PHOTOGRAPHS APPEAR COURTESY OF
THE GEORGE BUSH PRESIDENTIAL LIBRARY AND MUSEUM

Book Design by
HSU+ASSOCIATES

RUGGED LAND WEBSITE ADDRESS: WWW.RUGGEDLAND.COM

MAY 2004

1 3 5 7 9 10 8 6 4 2

FIRST EDITION

RUGGED LAND | 276 CANAL STREET · FIFTH FLOOR · NEW YORK CITY · NY 10013 · USA

" The best of... "

"I am probably the only mom in America who knows exactly what her son is doing and where he is doing it."

"I married the first man I ever kissed. When I tell this to my children, they just about throw up."

"My absolute favorite [speaking engagement]: The National Association of Plastic Surgeons. I was scared to death, I thought they were going to rush the stage!"

Asked whether she'd be willing to debate Hillary Clinton during the 1992 presidential race, she said, "Are you crazy? She'd win hands down. A debater I am not. Wrestling, maybe."

About Nancy Reagan: "As you know, we have a lot in common. She adores her husband; I adore mine. She fights drugs; I fight illiteracy. She wears a size three—so's my leg."

"Now that I'm the mother of a president, I can say almost anything I want and get away with it."

"What happens in the White House doesn't matter half as much as what happens in your house."

"People are like crayons," she said. "Some are sharp, some are dull, some have odd names, and they're all different colors, but they have to learn to live together in the same box."

"If I could give people one piece of advice, it would be, 'Never go up to someone and say that you didn't vote for her husband.'"

"I am advising the former president, the governor of Florida, and the president of the United States—I guess you could say I rule the world."

About the TV show *Survivor*: "George and I know what it's like to be voted off the island."

"You can't hide a piece of broccoli in a glass of milk; now, that would be very funny if I was talking about a grandchild."

First Mom

S he may not be glamorous, and she may not often make headlines, but Barbara Pierce Bush is probably one of the more influential women in American history. The wife of one president, the mother of another, and a direct descendant of the fourteenth president, Franklin Pierce, Barbara Bush has lived a life immersed in the world of politics. Yet she has captured the hearts of the American people by remaining down-to-earth and genuine, and by demonstrating a remarkable ability to poke fun at herself and the trappings of high office. Over the years, Barbara Bush's wit and wisdom have amused, enlightened, and touched even the most jaded among us—Republicans and Democrats alike. She really is, as she once put it, "everybody's grandmother." Barbara Bush is our nation's First Mom—white hair, fake pearls, wrinkles, struggling with her weight—and we love her all the more.

The Life of
Barbara Pierce Bush

Growing Up

arbara Pierce made her first political appearance on June 8, 1925, in Rye, New York, in the arms of her father, Marvin, a publishing executive, and her mother, Pauline, daughter of an Ohio supreme court justice. Though the country was in the midst of the Great Depression, Barbara grew up in relative luxury—a five-bedroom house on a quarter acre of land—but she struggled to compete for her mother's affection, often losing out to her older and more beautiful sister, Martha, or her younger brother, Scott, who had a serious medical condition. "My mother, I'm sure, was tired and irritable and I didn't understand at the time," Barbara has said. "But I guess I felt neglected that she didn't spend as much time on me. She had this enormous responsibility, which I was never sympathetic about. Now, as a mother and grandmother, I realize what she was going through."

Home for Christmas in 1941 from boarding school at Ashley Hall in Charleston, South Carolina, Barbara attended a dance and laid eyes for the first time on the man she would eventually marry. "I could hardly breathe when he was in the room," she remembered. It was love at first sight. George Herbert Walker Bush, the handsome and athletic son of a United States senator, was about to graduate from the prestigious Phillips Academy in Andover, Massachusetts, when he met the sixteen-year-old Barbara. After graduation, he joined the navy as a seaman second class, and, writing letters home constantly to his new sweetheart, he spent a year training at camps across the country before earning his ensign's bars and heading off to war. Prior to leaving he proposed to Barbara, and she happily accepted. George spent most of 1944 flying combat missions against the Japanese in the South Pacific but came home for Christmas, and two weeks later, on January 6, 1945, Barbara Pierce became Barbara Bush and their lives together began.

Barbara Bush

After the war ended, the newlyweds moved to New Haven, Connecticut, while George attended Yale University. Barbara gave birth to future Texas governor and United States president George Walker Bush on July 6, 1946. After graduating from Yale in 1948, George moved the family to Texas to take a chance in the oil business. More children followed: Pauline Robinson ("Robin") in 1949, named after Barbara's mother, who had died just two months earlier in a car accident; James Ellis ("Jeb"), future governor of Florida, in 1953; Neil in 1955; Marvin in 1956; and Dorothy ("Doro") in 1959. In 1953 tragedy struck when Robin died of leukemia at age three. Her death would leave Barbara and George with a lifelong compassion. "Because of Robin," she once said, "George and I love every living human more."

As Barbara stayed home raising the children, George built a series of successful oil businesses—keeping him on the road more than the couple would have liked but providing the financial cushion they would need for George's entrance into the world of politics.

First Mom

In 1962 George ran his first race—for chairman of the Harris County (Texas) Republican party. Barbara discovered—to her surprise and delight—that she really enjoyed being involved in the day-to-day grind of the campaign and helping to rouse support for her husband. After fifteen years focused on her children, the change of pace energized and excited her, and her ability to charm people—and remember their names and faces with startling accuracy—served George well. He won the race, and went on to run two years later for the United States Senate. Although George lost to the incumbent Democrat Ralph Yarborough, the defeat did not deter him. In 1966 he ran for the House of Representatives and became the first Republican ever elected in Harris County. When he was reelected without opposition in 1968, Texas Republican leaders and President Richard Nixon encouraged George to try again for the Senate in 1970. Despite a well-fought campaign, he lost once again, this time to Democrat Lloyd Bentsen, who would later run against Bush as Michael Dukakis's running mate in the 1988 presidential election.

After encouraging George to run for the Senate, only to see him lose, President Nixon appointed Bush the United States ambassador to the United Nations as a consolation prize. He and Barbara would have the opportunity to live in New York (at the glitzy Waldorf-Astoria hotel), and, with Doro the only child still living at home, after four years in Washington, D.C., the Bushes said yes and packed their bags.

In 1974, after a short stint as chairman of the Republican National Committee, President Ford asked George to serve as chief of the United States Liaison Office in Beijing, China. Barbara could not have been more excited about the opportunity, as it meant getting to spend extended time alone with her husband—in a country halfway around the world. The Bushes enjoyed their time in China tremendously, but it did not last long. In late 1975 President Ford asked George to return to the United States and serve as director of the CIA.

George jumped at the chance to help restore the agency's sagging morale after the Watergate scandal, but Barbara felt less enthusiastic. George's new job meant long hours and, due to the nature of the agency, the inability to share details of his work as he always had. Barbara felt lonely and isolated and fell into depression. Putting her energies into volunteer work helped her recover, as did the excitement of a brand-new campaign when George resigned from the CIA in 1977 and began working toward a bid for the 1980 Republican presidential nomination.

Barbara traveled the road almost daily campaigning for her husband and fought hard to help him win crucial primaries. And although the party eventually nominated former California governor Ronald Reagan as its candidate, Barbara's efforts helped put George in the position to be chosen as Reagan's running mate. The Reagan–Bush ticket beat incumbent president Jimmy Carter in a landslide, and Barbara found herself Second Lady. She was delighted to have a prominent platform to promote literacy, her chosen cause (the Bushes' son Neil was dyslexic, so this was a close and personal issue for Barbara), and although sometimes overshadowed by the more glamorous First Lady, Nancy Reagan, Barbara began to win the hearts of Americans with her disarming wit and common sense wisdom.

After eight years in the vice-presidential mansion, George moved down the street upon winning the 1988 presidential election, and Barbara was thrust into the spotlight as First Lady. She quickly established the Barbara Bush Foundation for Family

18   Literacy and helped push for passage of the 1991 Literacy Act. She advocated for the homeless, AIDS victims, the elderly, leukemia research, and school volunteer programs. And her popularity soared after she wrote two bestselling books about the family's dogs: *C. Fred's Story* and *Millie's Book*.

Since leaving the White House in 1992, Barbara has continued to fight for the causes most dear to her heart, and with her sons embarking on political careers of their own, she found herself back on the campaign trail—for Jeb in his successful race for governor of Florida, and for George W. in Texas, and then throughout the country in support of his successful run for president in 2000. From First Lady to First Mom, Barbara has proven herself steadfast in her devotion to her family and has made an indelible mark on the character of our country.

Barbara Bush

On Herself

"I've known for years that I was the luckiest woman in the world. I do have the most marvelous husband, children, and grandchildren. We live in the greatest country in the world."

"People have been very kind to me, and nobody's jealous of me, which is an accomplishment unto itself. Being married to the president is not actually a personal accomplishment. But I was lucky enough to marry well. I was the right person in the right place at the right time."

On being asked all sorts of questions about herself all the time, she noted: "We grew up in a world where you didn't talk about yourself all the time."

"Nobody had a happier childhood than I did. Nobody. To grow up in Rye, New York, in the 1930s was just the happiest existence in the world."

"I grew up in a family where every time I went out, if I acted slightly high-hat, my father would say, 'Just remember it is nice to be natural and you are naturally nice.' I learned quickly, Don't be something you are not. If I have a fault, I think I'm too relaxed."

"I grew up in a house with no TV and no radio; we didn't have those distractions. My father worked for the largest publishing company in the country at the time, and each week, he brought home the magazines they printed, like *National Geographic* and *Reader's Digest,* along with a few they didn't print, like the *Saturday Evening Post.* They had serials, so I would read those. I was always third in line to get them, behind my mother and sister, but that's how we spent our time: We sat around and read."

Barbara Bush

"My dad commuted to New York and he didn't bring his business home with him. I knew nothing about the publishing business, but I grew up with McCall's pattern books because we waited for the outdated one. He brought it home and we cut out new dolls every year. All my little friends made dresses for them. We'd put them on cardboard and we had our little families and put clothes on them. With that big McCall's pattern book, I was the envy of the neighborhood."

On her most famous ancestor, President Franklin Pierce, she said, "The only thing I remember about him was years ago as a child, reading that he was one of our weakest presidents. I was humiliated."

Her grades suffered when she went to Smith College. "I didn't like to study too much. I'd hate to have anybody go through my records from freshman year. I was all right in high school, but when it came to Smith, I was a cliff-hanger. The truth is, I just wasn't very interested. I was just interested in George…."

In their one-room apartment in Wyandotte, Michigan, where she lived with George in the early years of their marriage, Barbara discovered that she didn't know how to keep house. "I ruined everything—and I mean everything. I shrank my whole trousseau. That was a weakness of my mother. She had a theory that if you could read, you could keep house."

"My piecrust is nothing to write home about."

When a reporter was being served cookies during their luncheon interview, Barbara pointed out, "Please. That's not my cookie recipe," referring to the famous one that was published earlier in *Family Circle.*

"All I ever did was marry and birth well."

Barbara Bush

"I spent all my life with my mother saying, 'Eat up, Martha' to my older sister, and 'Not you, Barbara.'"

When Barbara was twelve, she weighed 148 pounds. "I looked like Porky Pig and probably should have gone to a diet camp."

When the media pointed out that Barbara would be going to three Thanksgiving dinners in Saudi Arabia to show support for and solidarity with the American troops there, she said, "You know, I was built for this job."

At a Lincoln Day banquet in Manchester, she confided she began the year 2000 with "the same New Year's resolution I've had every year as long as I can remember. Can you guess what it is?" Then she turned her back to the crowd and placed her hands on her hips. "I haven't had a call from Jenny Craig."

First Mom

"I am the world's most disciplined soul except for one thing—food. I write all my letters. I keep my diary, pay my bills, fix the scrapbook, I'm just very disciplined. But I just fall apart when it comes to food."

As to what kinds of foods she truly relished, she said, "Just anything. That's how I deal with tension. I just go eat something. It's like, 'That will show that person who said that ugly thing.'"

In an interview with Barbara Walters on television, she said, "George said to me, 'You don't want that dessert, do you? Do you?' And I said, 'Well, I have to eat it, George, for my fans.'"

During the Bushes' Florida post-election vacation, photos of her swimming in the type of bathing suit popular with matrons in the fifties appeared; the campaigning had added thirteen pounds to her five-foot-eight-inch frame. Later, she jokingly begged photographers to cap their lenses: "My children are complaining all over the country."

Barbara Bush

"It's not easy being the wife of the president. Last Sunday a reader of *Parade* magazine wrote in with one of those burning questions....She wrote: 'I would like to know how much Barbara Bush weighs,' and they answered it. *Parade* magazine says I weigh between one hundred and thirty-five and one hundred and forty pounds. George said, 'The press never gets anything right.' Just for starters, I was born weighing one hundred and thirty-five pounds."

At a topless beach in the Greek Isles: "I am shocked, not by the nude bodies, but by the FAT old nude bodies. UGLY."

"[A] letter that truly thrilled me and amused my family came from a dear little girl who said something like: 'Dear Mrs. Bush, Great news! I've named my heifer after you.'"

"When I let it go white, one of my boys said to me, 'Oh, Mother, why did you dye your hair?' I thought, The kid thinks I dyed my hair white."

On the days before she stopped coloring her hair: "I began coloring it myself, but it turned every color but the warm brown I wanted. So back when George was running for the Senate, I went to the beauty parlor and said how bad my hair looked. The beautician said, 'Let's try this rinse called Fabulous Fawn.' So we rinsed with Fabulous Fawn and off I flew to East Texas to campaign....It was a hundred and five degrees in that plane. I asked the pilot to turn up the air-conditioning, but he told me it had just gone out. And my Fabulous Fawn began to run. It ran down my neck, my ears, my cheeks, and my forehead. I began to blot myself with Kleenex, used all that up, then started on toilet paper. I spent the whole flight mopping myself up....Finally I decided to stick with my gray."

Barbara Bush

"I wash my hair every day of my life and probably washed all the color out. But I can exercise, play tennis. I don't ever have to say to George, 'I'm sorry, I can't do that, I just got my hair done.' You have to have priorities in life, and that's just not one I have. What you see is what you get."

When people suggested that she dye her white hair a "younger" shade, she said, "It makes me mad as the dickens. If I did something like that, I think all of America would fall flat on its face from astonishment."

After getting one letter too many about why she didn't dye her hair, she finally began sending back a standard response: "I said, 'Please forget about my hair. Think about my wonderful mind.'"

Barbara decided to play a little April Fools' joke in 1989 by donning a strawberry-blond wig at a huge gathering at the Gridiron Club. "The color could have been a little lighter, but then I wasn't going for a beauty contest. [The idea] just struck me. It was something that amused me…I thought, I'm just tired of the hair, talking about it. I'll just wear a wig and see how they like me in that."

Of a family gathering she said, "One of the brothers took a poll of all the family members to see who had the grayest hair, and he said I won."

Barbara Bush

Someone had suggested that Barbara get a makeover to look younger. "When George was first going to run for president, a member of our family said, 'What are we going to do about Barbara?' I said, 'Funny, it doesn't bother George Bush.'"

She told audiences once about how a child who had seen her speak talked about seeing George Washington's mother. "That would be funny, except I look a little bit like him," she said.

"My absolute favorite [speaking engagement]: The National Association of Plastic Surgeons. I was scared to death," she said. "I thought they were going to rush the stage!"

"It's the gray-haired ladies who come up and say, 'Gee, you look exactly like my mother' who worry me a bit. But I don't mind. The truth is, if I've learned nothing in my thousand years, I've learned that you really shouldn't judge a book by its cover."

First Mom

She once wrote in her weekly campaign diary for *USA Today:* "What I would like to tell [the woman who suggested that Barbara got her wrinkles from sleeping on the pillow wrong] is that the wrinkles came not from sleeping but from not getting any sleep at all."

"The worst [photograph] of me came out in Detroit. You could have planted a whole potato field in the rows of wrinkles."

Of the numerous pictures taken of her during her years as First Lady, Barbara said, "Unfortunately, my winning smile makes me look as if I'm being electrocuted. My kids are always looking at photographs of me and saying, 'Look at Mom, she's plugged in again!'"

After pointing out the holiday decorations all over the White House in 1991, many of which were handmade needlepoint ornaments that looked like Barbara Bush, she said, "There are a lot of white-haired, fat, pearled ones."

Barbara Bush

At a salute held in her honor at the Kennedy Center during Inauguration Week, she came onstage, turned around slowly like a model, and told the audience: "Please notice: hairdo, makeup, designer dress. Look at me good this week, because it's the only week of my life you're ever going to see it."

First Mom

"People can be so rude about the fact that George looks so young and I look so old. It's not nice."

"I'm not going to turn into a glamorous princess. I'm not going to worry about it. I have plenty of self-confidence, not in how I look but in how I feel, and I feel good about my husband, my children, and my life."

Barbara wrote a letter in response to a story in *The Wichita Eagle* in which a journalist mistakenly said that she had had three breast sizes—rather than "dress sizes"—during her life.

To the Editor:

I've just become abreast of your recent article "Barbara Bush Wows El Dorado." I very much enjoyed my recent visit to Butler County Community College and enjoyed reading about it in *The Wichita Eagle*, but alas, I must inform you of a misquote regarding my speech. I am indeed a bosom buddy to two presidents, so I shared some

Barbara Bush

of the things I have learned in seventy-six years of life. That includes fifty-seven years of married life, six children, fourteen grandchildren, five wars, three DRESS sizes, two governors, two parachute jumps, and now two presidents. Your article has left this generally outspoken mother speechless, but has given my children much to laugh about.

Warmly,
Barbara Bush

At the end of the typed letter was a handwritten note: "I just wanted to get this off my chest!"

"Lots of people want to redo me. My favorite so far was the lady who took the *Life* magazine picture, gave me a new haircut, new earrings, necklace, clothes, makeup, and sent me a slide she had taken of her work of art."

On her infamous pearls, she confessed, "They're all different and they're all fake."

"There's a myth going around that I don't dress well. I dress very well—I just don't look so good."

A journalist told her, "Miniskirts are coming back, and various people have noticed that your skirts were a little shorter on your recent visit to Paris." She said, "Shorter, yes. But no shorter than this. I've gone as high as I'm going."

On a cruise on the Bosporus strait, she wore one red sneaker and one blue. She claimed that George "gave me twenty pairs for my birthday. How else will

I ever wear them all? Now I'm the Imelda Marcos of
Kennebunkport."

She imparted a few words of advice on comp-
limenting people on their clothes. "Think twice
about criticizing someone's clothes. What they
change into could be tighter and shorter than what
they took off."

When she made the official announcement that she had Graves' disease, also known as hyperthyroidism, which would require radiation treatment, she told the reporters, "Now, please, don't have me dying."

After being treated to a complete round of radiation therapy for her hyperthyroid condition, which had been causing her double vision, she revealed, "So far everybody says I've been just angelic. I haven't changed a bit. I'm just as mean as ever."

She felt that her fatigue was caused by her hyperthyroid condition. "I'm lucky if I get through the days. I don't mean I'm overextended, but I am sixty-three years old and I need to be babied a bit."

Barbara Bush

Shortly after becoming First Lady at the age of sixty-four, she said of her appearance, "I'm so old now that I don't have to pretend to be something I'm not."

Prior to her sixty-fifth birthday, she requested no birthday cards or anything of the sort: "I walk around like Scrooge in this house, saying, 'Anyone who mentions it, I'll cut off your head.'"

She exercised in the private pool in the White House, usually with a Secret Service agent watching. "Someone watches me swim a mile every day. Talk about watching the grass grow."

In her early days as Second Lady, she got a lot of letters. "When we first got into office, someone wrote and said, 'Dear Mrs. Bush: This is a youthful administration. The vice president looks young, Mrs. Reagan looks young. Why don't you?' I wrote back: 'I'm doing the best I can. And besides, I'm the youngest of all those people.'"

First Mom

When Barbara Bush replaced Nancy Reagan as First Lady, a *New York Post* headline proclaimed, "Goodbye, First Fashion Plate—Hello, First Grandmother." Her reaction at the time: "My mail tells me a lot of fat, white-haired, wrinkled ladies are tickled pink."

She mentioned that she and George have already signed up to donate their organs upon death. "Well, what do I want them for? I don't feel squeamish about that. I don't think I've got anything that's useful, but anything I've got, they can use it for research as far as I'm concerned."

"I'd like to think of myself as 'national teenager,' but I don't believe I'm going to get away with that. I might even go for 'national mother.'"

On the importance of being a role model to other senior citizens, she said, "I mean, look at me—if I can be a success, so can they."

"George and I have so many new body parts, we're afraid God won't recognize us if we get to heaven!"

Barbara Bush

While campaigning on behalf of her son Jeb, who was running for the governorship of Florida, Barbara admitted, "One sure sign of age is when you suddenly realize your children are wiser than you."

"Very few people dare to call me a senior citizen."

On her popularity, she observed, "Who dislikes being liked? Of course it's baloney. I mean, people—if they do like me, Barbara [Barbara Grizzuti Harrison, the journalist who was interviewing her]—like me as I am, and it isn't tough to live up to that. You don't have to live up to nothing. Here I am." With that she flung arms wide. "Nothing. If people thought I was beautiful, brilliant, glamorous, and all those things, it might be a tad of a problem. But people don't think that of me. What do they think? That I'm their neighbor. They know everything about me. Everything. They know I love my husband. They know I love my children. They know I love my God. They know I love my country and I adore my life. I'm

Barbara Bush

First Mom

not smarter than anybody else, I'm not dumber than anybody else; I am loved."

Someone asked her once: "Mrs. Bush, I'm a big admirer of yours. And my question for you is what—if you would have finished your college education— what would have been your career if things at the time were different?"

BARBARA BUSH: I understand. I'm not sure; I suspect I would have majored in, you know, English or something; but I wanted to be sort of a nurse later. I mean, I worked in hospitals for many years as a volunteer, and I think that's where some of my talents lay, at that time anyway. I like to be with sick people if you can make them feel better.

"George used to tell me, years ago, 'You've got to tell people that's a joke. People don't know.' My sense of humor is very different. But I only kid people I like. That's a good rule of thumb. If I don't like someone, I'm apt to not kid at all or freeze over slightly. But there are very few people I don't like. I can't think of any."

Barbara Bush

"I'm not a competitive person, and I think women like me because they don't think I'm competitive, just nice."

Asked what qualities she sought in a friend, she said, "I don't look for anything. I often find loyalty, humor, goodness. Hope they find the same from me."

"I'm a big kisser and you can see people turning a cheek instead, afraid I'm going to get 'em!"

"I take several baths a day."

"Nobody ever said I was a saint."

"I'm neither better nor worse than anybody else."

At a speech at the Barbara Bush Elementary School, Barbara used the name often. "I like to say the name of this school. I think it has a certain ring to it."

Living a
Political Life

"L osing [a political race] is very painful. Maybe more painful for the wife than the husband."

When her husband first brought up the idea of leaving New Haven, Connecticut, for Odessa, Texas, she was against it. But in hindsight on the move to Texas, she said, "I didn't want to go at the time. But a day after I got there, I thought it was really exciting....If we had been bound by our past, we'd have stayed in Greenwich or Rye and done our thing like everybody else in our family did. But we ventured out."

During the 1950s, living in a development back in Midland, Texas, was wonderful. "It was just the right time to live there. I remember Dad visiting us in Midland and saying, 'I worry about you. What

if something happened? Who would support you?'
Well, we were all in the same situation. No one had
any family. We were all newcomers and we came
from all over the country. We formed really good
friendships."

On making do with what the Bushes had in their
early days in Texas, she remembered that "as we had
the only bathroom on the street, we didn't complain."

On raising their children in Texas, she remembered,
"There were very dormant years in there where I
was perfectly happy to have children. I always did
volunteer work, but I didn't do anything imaginative
or creative. George was building businesses all
around the world, and we couldn't afford for me to
go to those places with him."

"I had moments where I was jealous of attractive
young women out in a man's world. I would think, well,
George is off on a trip doing all these exciting things
and I'm sitting home with these absolutely brilliant
children who say one thing a week of interest."

Barbara Bush

On the years in Congress, she said, "He loved the Congress, but I suspect he found it very frustrating. It moves slowly and sometimes not at all. A congressman has about 450,000 constituents, all of whom think you are as close as your telephone. I'll never forget the night our phone rang at four A.M. and a fuzzy voice said, 'Sorry to call you at this hour, George, but I thought this was a good time to catch you at home.'"

Barbara Bush was overlooked during the beginning of her husband's political career, and she confided in a reporter that if she ever wrote a book, it would be called *Will the Woman in the Red Dress Please Get Out of the Picture*. According to her, that's what a photographer had yelled during a rally where she stood next to her husband. "I looked down at my dress and I thought, 'My Lord, it's me.'"

She often went with her husband to Security Council meetings when he was the United States ambassador to the United Nations. "You try not to sit with someone your husband's going to vote against.

But if it does happen, nobody bats an eyelash. They're a very sophisticated crowd."

On George's United Nations job, she said, "I would pay to have this job. It was like being taken around the world to meet people from 128 countries and yet never having to pack a bag or sleep in a strange bed."

When President Nixon asked George to run the Republican National Committee, Barbara discovered that her husband was expected to handle damage control as more and more revelations about Nixon surfaced during the Watergate scandal. "It was like a leaky roof, where you're running around with pots, trying to stop the water. George used to say it was like being married to a centipede, and it kept dropping shoes."

When George became the first top-level diplomat stationed at the United States mission in Beijing, Barbara was ecstatic. It "was a whole new leaf in both our lives. Watergate was a terrible experience, so to go off to China and learn a whole new culture was beautiful. I loved the people. I loved the whole feeling."

On being with George in those days in Beijing, she said, "I loved it there. I had George all to myself."

She suffered a deep depression when she was less involved with her husband's career once he became the director of the CIA. "Sometimes the pain was so great, I felt the urge to drive into a tree or an oncoming car."

On her depression, she reflected, "All my children were gone, so it was the empty-nest syndrome. And George had a new job that I couldn't share—and he's the most heavenly man about sharing. But I'm just not a good secret-keeper. My famous last words are 'Don't tell George I told you, but...'"

She admitted in a letter to a friend after George assumed the helm of the CIA: "I shall curl up every time I read or hear a mean word about George, and he tells me that in this new job I'll see and hear a heck of a lot!"

She blamed politics for her feelings of inadequacy during her six-month depression in 1976. "Suddenly women's lib had made me feel my life had been wasted."

She talked about her depression on the TV program Larry King Live.

LARRY KING: The job of his, it appears, that you like the least was CIA.

BARBARA BUSH: Well, that's because I can't keep a secret; I'm going to tell you the honest truth. And I—I mean, we discussed it, and we both know I can't keep a secret.

LARRY: So he didn't tell you?

BARBARA: I asked him not to tell me, but he did share with me. But, you know, you're talking about the depression I had. I really—it was stupid of me, Larry. I'm glad now I—

LARRY: What do you mean, it's stupid? You can't control it.

Barbara: No, but I could've gotten help, but I was too sort of proud to get help. And when George—he was the only person I told. I didn't tell Andy...my closest friend in the world; I didn't tell anybody.

During her years as Second Lady, she calculated how she spent her days. "I spend fifty percent of my time doing charitable work and twenty-five percent on organizational things like running the house. Maybe fifteen percent on my husband and children and maybe ten percent on myself, exercising and playing tennis."

When George brought up his fear of losing the 1988 presidential race, he said he wanted to get into a car and drive right out of Washington after the inauguration. She pointed out to him that he had the services of a chauffeur. "I said, 'You'll leave by yourself because I'm not leaving the White House in a car with a man who's never driven in eight years.'"

A reporter once asked her whether she had gone shopping for an inauguration dress even though the votes weren't in yet. She said, "No. I didn't name my babies until I had them in my arms, and it was clearly obvious I was having them."

Of their walks during George's inaugural parade as president, Barbara said, "We walked maybe three times, five minutes—not enough. You know, it's so frustrating riding in a car that's going two miles an hour. You know you can walk faster than that."

"People feel good at any inauguration, not just ours. People feel good about their country, about a change of leadership. I don't know if it's because we're so secure that we don't feel threatened or that people love the people who've been elected. But anyway, there was a feeling of just a great day."

She once caught photographers waiting directly below her bedroom window. "I had to crawl to my closet to get my clothes."

"One morning [at a spa on a cruise] George was coming out of the shower toweling off when a man approached him with a camera saying: 'Do you mind if I take your picture?' George, dripping wet and stark naked, suggested that the time was not quite right."

When the Bushes learned that a new hospital wing would have a plaque that said Barbara had dedicated the wing "on the occasion of the visit to Paris of George Bush," she turned to the crowd, and said, "I'm going to show you that I learned something from my husband in Hungary. I'm going to give up my speech and just tell you that speaking from the heart, as he did, this is one of the nicest things that ever could happen to me, and selfishly, I feel like you've stretched my life a little bit because now I'm on a plaque."

On what it meant to be president, she remarked from observing her husband: "You know you're not away in this job no matter where you are. George even talked to one head of state from aboard the boat."

Just after her husband vomited into the lap of the Japanese prime minister Kiichi Miyazawa, she helped wipe the vomit from his lips. After George was taken away, she chose to stay behind and put the rest of the stunned room at ease. "You know, I can't explain what happened to George, because it's never happened before. But I'm beginning to think it's the ambassador's fault." She acknowledged Michael Armacost, the United States ambassador to Japan. "He and George played the emperor and the crown prince in tennis today and they were badly beaten. And we Bushes aren't used to that. So he felt much worse than I thought."

She remembers one occasion when she accompanied her husband on various diplomatic functions. "We had a night where you charge from reception to reception. I'd worn a short bright-red cocktail suit with gold threads. It could not have been redder—or louder. After three receptions, I said, 'Where to now?' George said, 'Come on, I'll tell you about it later.' And we raced up some stairs. Next thing we knew, we were in a funeral parlor. The ambassador of a Central American country had died. All the ladies were properly dressed in black and I was there in bright red. We were thrust into the center of the lights as the television announcer said, 'And here

comes the United States ambassador and Mrs. Bush.'
I couldn't wait to get out of there."

On whether her husband would run for reelection, she told CBS in August 1991 that "it had to do with, will I still be able to bend over and work in my garden when he gets out of office or will we be able to travel with our grandchildren or will George be able to take me down the Inland Waterway in a boat, that kind of thing, selfish things."

Eventually she decided that "I don't think I can be that selfish."

She ultimately supported her husband's decision to run for reelection. "The truth is, I think he has to run."

She gloated a little about her accomplishments during the 1992 presidential race. "Don't discount me. I've written two books. I've raised wonderful children. I've raised hundreds of thousands of dollars."

"I am advising the former president, the governor of Florida, and the president of the United States—I guess you could say I rule the world."

Barbara Bush

Campaigning
and Politics

"You're looking at a lady who cast her first vote for 'President Thomas Dewey.'"

"The first time I campaigned, I probably lost George hundreds of votes. I'm not only outspoken, I'm honest."

When asked by a student to give advice for budding politicians, she said, "I have the most unpopular answer for that. Before anyone runs for office, they need to get a job, feed their family, build a life, build a cathedral if need be. Then you can go be a politician, because you'll know what it's like to fill out a job application, work for a living, produce something."

On campaigning: "Some days I loved it and some days I hated it. Sometimes I was so tired, as is every candidate—candidate and wife—that I just thought, I can't move. The hotel windows don't open and the motels have hard beds and they all smell like cigarette smoke—some days. Some days you're in the most beautiful places in the world."

"In order to be able to survive what a campaign does to you, you have to sometimes stick your head in the sand, like an ostrich, and block it out."

"George doesn't like me to say it because it makes you sound like a nincompoop when you say you don't follow the news. But...it's just hard to go out and campaign for twelve hours when you're hearing such depressing things."

When her husband lost his Senate bid in 1964, she said, "He was wonderful. He got right on the phone the next morning and thanked everybody who helped him, you know, cheering them up. I was terrible. I went out and played tennis and tears were flowing down my face."

Barbara Bush

On disagreeing with her husband in public: "No, no.
I muzzled myself about 1967 when George went into
the Congress. It's a decision I made many years ago that
when I disagreed with George Bush, I tell him in private.
Occasionally I've had slippage, but very rarely."

The 1980 Reagan–Bush campaign provided a
lot of fond memories for Barbara. "I liked it for a
lot of reasons, not the end result, but I liked the
campaigning. I felt I was really helping George. I
probably lost votes by the hundreds, but I thought I
was helping. The children and I all got much closer
to each other and to George. Every one of them did
their part, and it's true that they now treat me as an
adult for the first time."

When a journalist from *The Detroit News* noticed
what Barbara was doing—needlepoint—on their
plane ride out of Iowa after her husband's successful
caucus vote, he said, "That's interesting. It looks like
a seat cover."

Barbara replied, "It's for George, and I'm leaving
the needle in it. He's got to keep moving."

62   During the period of suspense before presidential
candidate Ronald Reagan would pick his running
mate in the summer of 1980, she observed that "it's
funny, everybody makes fun of the job, but everybody
I knew there wanted it."

"I do not agree with my husband on everything,
and I am not going to tell you if I don't agree,"
Barbara Bush once told *The New York Times* during
the first Reagan–Bush campaign. "Because I am
going to tell George Bush how I feel. Upstairs."

In an interview Cokie Roberts conducted for
Seventeen magazine, she asked Barbara: "I'm the
child of politicians myself, and I think it's always
harder on the family than it is on the candidate,
particularly when a campaign gets rough. Has it
been hard?"

BARBARA BUSH: Yes, I think it is harder on the
family. I take it very seriously. We're all laughing
because our shy little daughter has now taken off the
gloves and is ready to fight. She does not like criticism
of her father. I think we all take it differently. I'd say

George [W.] and Dorothy are right in there. Neil takes it as a challenge. Jeb can't wait to fight. Really Marvin and I are the sissies, and the others are kind of feisty.

Her intense dislike of Jane Pauley, the *Today Show* interviewer, is no big secret and can be traced to this one question Ms. Pauley asked her: "Mrs. Bush, people say George is a man for the eighties and you're a woman of the forties. What do you say to that?" Even though she felt like crying, she said, "If you mean I love my family, my country, and my God, so be it."

George Bush admitted that he had been instructed to "be a little more demonstrative" as part of his campaign strategy in the 1988 presidential race. When he finally introduced her at a speech, Barbara gave her husband an exaggerated hug. "Thank you very, very much, sweetie." Then she turned to the audience. "See if he looks at me as adoringly as I looked at him."

On her reputed role as a key campaign adviser

during the 1988 presidential race, Barbara explained her role at periodic briefing sessions in Kennebunkport: "George asked me to come in because I'm going to have to feed [campaign aides] and house them. I said to Craig [Fuller, George Bush's chief of staff], 'I promise you they'll have clean sheets, clean windows to look out of. I will feed them. I hope I can sit in on the meetings.' He said, 'Well, we can't change now'—he was kidding me."

In her weekly campaign diary she wrote for *USA Today* in the late 1980s, she shared a story about her travels. "I had a small crisis this week. I was staying at a very stylish hotel in New York City, where I knew they always had a bathrobe in the closet, so I left mine at home. I had called room service for coffee, then discovered there was no robe. When the coffee came, I took a sheet off the bed and wrapped it around myself toga-style to answer the door. I can just imagine what the waiter thought. I can just see him going back downstairs to the kitchen and saying, 'You'll never guess what I saw in Room 1712!'"

Barbara Bush

In the *Newsweek* cover story "George Bush: Fighting the 'Wimp Factor'" in October 1987, she said, "It was a cheap shot. It hurt. It hurt our children, truthfully. It hurt George's mother. It hurt me. I mean, it was hurtful."

After being asked about her husband's "wimp factor" over and over again, Barbara said, "I'm not going to answer that question anymore, as of this moment. I never want to hear that word again. Any other questions?"

"Nobody mentions the many good things that George did: the Clean Air Act; the biggest Civil Rights Bill ever—the Americans with Disabilities Act, which improved the lives of 40 million Americans; The National Literacy Act of 1991, the first bill of its kind, which helped give the literacy cause some much-needed national focus; and the economy, which was growing at 5 percent when he turned it over to Bill Clinton.... But the greatest thing he did was teach us how to keep the peace by staying close to our allies. So when Saddam Hussein invaded

Kuwait, George was able to form a worldwide coalition, assemble an enormous force in Saudi Arabia, and—after trying every peaceful means—win a war against this aggressor and drive him out of Kuwait."

When asked whether she took her children along on the campaign trail, she said: "No, unless we went to a family picnic or something. But we really didn't involve them. I was very protective of them, and we tried to keep their lives as normal as possible. For many many years, George Bush and I never went out on Sunday, I mean ever. We went to church on Sunday, but we never went out unless they were invited. Those days are gone, but now they all come home to us on Sundays."

Larry King once asked her, "Are you uncomfortable in a broadcast setting or an interview setting?"

Her response? "A little bit; I feel sort of feisty, and I hate that. I'm not a—you know, I feel like, what are we doing in a campaign? George Bush is the most qualified man; he's done more for America than any

president's ever done; and how could we even be in
this kind of campaign?"

Once, on the way to her interviews at the 1988
Republican Convention, she came across a news
reporter she knew sleeping soundly on the floor.
"I stopped for a moment and wrote him a note that
said, 'I came by to give you an interview. Sorry I
missed you.' Then I signed my name and left it on his
tummy."

On the popularity of wives eclipsing that of their
politician husbands, she quipped, "How come we're
not presidents?"

"I don't read the papers. I won't watch TV. I won't
do any of that. But I will vote three or four times."

When asked whether she'd be willing to debate
Hillary Clinton during the 1992 presidential race,
she said, "Are you crazy? She'd win hands down. A
debater I am not. Wrestling, maybe."

Instead of criticizing Hillary Clinton's choosing to have a career rather than to "bake cookies," she said, "Everybody's different and that's a great thing. We're talking about two men, and I've got the better candidate."

On the escalated mudslinging—particularly concerning her husband's alleged infidelities—in the presidential race of 1992, Barbara said to a journalist, "You need to know about character, you don't need to know about sex. How can anyone know about her sex life [pointing at Anna Perez, her press secretary]…? Character, though—are you loyal, are you true to your commitments, do you keep your word, do you do your best, are you decent?—that counts with me. But that other—sex—I don't want to get into that other.…An outrage."

"History is being written by gossip, untruths, half-truths, and mistakes passed along by unreliable websites. Anyone can start their own website and many have. I have more people tell me something they've heard, and I'll say, 'How interesting. That's not true.'

Barbara Bush

Then they'll tell me they saw it on the Internet."

69

When confronted with a *New York Post* story saying George had had an affair with aide Jennifer Fitzgerald while he was vice president, she said, "It is ugly and the press ought to be ashamed of themselves, printing something that is a lie. I felt the same way—I don't have a double standard—about printing the Bill Clinton story, from a woman who was paid" to tell her story. Clinton "never denied he had a fling, did he? That doesn't mean George Bush should be smeared with the same brush when he didn't."

Because Ms. Fitzgerald was out of the country at the time when the story was published, she added, "I haven't seen Jennifer, but my heart goes out to her. This is just mean."

"Character's an issue if you're talking about cheating, lying, deceiving, maybe not keeping vows—I don't know, those are important things. But you don't come out when there's no proof and you don't smear good men and women when there's no proof. That's just ugly, and it's not all the news that's fit to print."

First Mom

"When you have a superb candidate of your own, I don't think you need to knock other people."

When she read the anti–Barbara Bush piece in *Vanity Fair* in which she was described as difficult and impossible, she said, "How do you get George Bush? Clobber his wife."

She had a conversation about George W.'s presidential campaign with the journalist Cokie Roberts on TV once.

COKIE ROBERTS: You told *USA Today* that President Bush is obsessed by this campaign.

BARBARA BUSH: He is, slightly.

COKIE: What does that mean?

BARBARA: Well, it means that I don't want to live with it all the time. My stomach is churning and I'm—I don't take criticism of my children very well. So you can imagine how much I like turning on the news all the time. He likes the twenty-four-hour station going. I don't mean—I'm not saying CNN, just any twenty-four-hour station going, and he's just interested in every poll. Well, I'm not, because I know that the right man's gonna win.

COKIE: And, and is he offering a lot of advice?

BARBARA: No. He really isn't. He's biting his lip and it's probably killing him.

When asked in 2000 whether she felt her campaigning could help her son George W. get elected president, she said, "There just is something, an aura, about having the former First Lady show up. It doesn't matter how bad she was, but, I mean, I think it makes a difference."

When asked why she was enjoying campaigning, this time for George W., she replied, "Because I can step in for two days and step out, number one. Number two, I really like my candidate."

Barbara Bush

Her Husband, George

A bout the first time Barbara saw George Bush, she said, "I could hardly breathe when he was in the room."

"So many great things have happened to me because I married well."

When she met George, she had a "nonkissing" boyfriend at the time but quickly scuttled him in favor of George. "I had a beau at the time and to show how lucky life can be, he now has had four wives. It's true, and all twenty years younger. I would have been gone long ago."

"I think he's the greatest man I ever knew. I wake up every single morning and look over at that funny old face and say, I'm the luckiest woman in the world.

That's lucky, isn't it?'"

"Love at first sight? No, no. I was a lot more lucky. I knew he was the most wonderful-looking man I ever saw, but I didn't think I knew what love was until we'd been married five years. I mean, I think I really loved him, but I don't think I really liked him. I'm not saying that the right way; didn't have the depth of love...I don't know how you know at nineteen...We were babies at nineteen." She clarified, "Not me. I was married."

"I do remember calling my family, saying that George and I were engaged. The family said, 'Oh, really?' It was so obvious to them we were in love that of course they didn't have to be told. It was sort of, 'How could you be so silly? We've known it all along.'" Barbara admitted that she felt hurt that her family had embraced her husband-to-be so completely. "They could have put up a little bit of a fight."

"Also, there was a war [World War II] going on. One has to remember that when you got engaged at that time you weren't sure you would ever see that person again when they went overseas. I know my mother and father really liked George, but I don't think they believed we would get married. I believe they were thinking they would take it one step at a time. George's parents probably felt the same way."

"I married the first man I ever kissed. When I tell this to my children, they just about throw up."

"George Bush sleeps with two girls." She paused. "Millie and me."

"The way George scolded [our children] was by silence or by saying, 'I'm disappointed in you.' And they would almost faint."

"In a marriage where one is so willing to take on responsibility and the other so willing to keep the bathroom clean, that's the way you get treated. Whenever there were any big decisions, the children always went to their father, probably because they'd always seen me as the—I hate to say—laundress, but

First Mom

as the nagging mother who said, 'Have you done your homework?'"

During the time of their daughter Robin's battle with leukemia, she remembered how her husband coped. "He was just killing himself, while I was very strong."

"I honestly don't think he's ever had a mean or ugly thought. I will say to him sometimes, 'I just wouldn't have so-and-so over for dinner. I mean, he not only didn't vote for you, he endorsed someone else,' and George will say, 'Move on. Isn't it better to have a friend than an enemy?' You can't make him be mean and ugly."

"[Disagreeing with George] is not a big deal, and if the question is do I think my husband's the greatest man that ever walked the earth, the answer is yes."

"George is not a good quarreler—he doesn't like to quarrel, he likes to discuss."

Barbara Bush

First Mom

"I'm not a good listener. I always think ahead and say, 'Well, you're wrong about that.' George thinks when you're asked a question, you're supposed to listen, then answer."

Was she always candid with her husband? "Oh, very candid. That's why we do so well. I tell him what I think, he tells me what he thinks. Then we are united."

"When he says 'I know what you're thinking,'" Barbara said, "I always say, 'I'm not thinking that.' But I am. He knows it too."

"A reporter once asked George what his proudest accomplishment was. He said that the kids still come home. He meant it."

"I think they are darn nice children, so I think whatever we did was all right. George has always put his family first. I mean, he's marvelous about any one of us who want to talk to George Bush. We don't just call and chat, but we know if we call his office

there?" or "Is Dad there?" he calls back within
fifteen or twenty minutes."

When told that she was the more popular half of
the First Couple, she said, "They ought to love George
Bush. He's the most wonderful man...We're talking
about apples and oranges and that's what really
counts. The orange is what counts. I'm the apple."

When someone yelled "We love you, Barbara" at
a speech she'd made, she fired back, "I want you to
love George."

When the journalist Donnie Radcliffe noted the
lack of affection between her and her husband
in public, Barbara said, "George is very, very
affectionate in private, but we are just not—"

George happened to be there. "Wait a minute." He
slid his left arm around her. "You saw me put my
arm around you."

"You know, we've been married so long, we don't
have to do that. It's fake."

"Sweetie," George said. "Let's go down life's highway together into the sunset."

She finally relented. "This is the way we sit and read books every night."

"He and I are very affectionate in our own way. We are the most happily married couple. We don't have to pretend for people."

George and Barbara found a way to amuse themselves when the speeches at dinner parties were a tad too long and dull. "Sometimes, well, almost all the time, there'll be an after-dinner speaker who reminds us of something funny. I look across at George and get laughing, 'cause he knows what I'm thinking and I know exactly how it's going to grab him." She added, "Of course, I hope other people laugh at us too."

On the media criticism of her husband, she admitted, "Occasionally, you wake up and there's terrible press. You think, why should such a wonderful man, why should he take all that?"

Barbara Bush

"[George] gives credit to others and never ever felt that he, alone, did anything. And, of course, he didn't. He assembled a great team. That takes genius[.]"

"You can criticize me, but don't criticize my children and don't criticize my daughters-in-law and don't criticize my husband, or you're dead."

When Barbara heard about Nancy Reagan consulting an astrologer about President Reagan's schedule, she said, "I'm a Gemini, so's George. We were told we probably should never get married, that Gemini don't get along. So I'll think about it—after forty-three years."

A woman in the audience admitted to Barbara that she'd met George Bush years ago and remembered him as "the sexiest man I've ever seen." Barbara chuckled, then turned sternly to the audience. "Anyone in this room who ever sees George Bush, don't you ever tell him that!"

First Mom

"I've always been a part of George Bush's life. He is a sharer. The role of a wife is to be supportive, and I've been very happy these thirty-five years. So don't rock my boat."

After watching Barbara try her hand at golf, the president told the press that her game "stunk." Later, when urged by journalists to play with her, he found an angry Barbara firing back. "When? Just like he's going to garden with me one day."

When rumors first surfaced about her husband's alleged affairs, Barbara wondered: "How can George Bush have an affair? He can't stay up past ten o'clock."

On George's leadership during the Persian Gulf War, she claimed, "I really was in awe of him."

As for the tradition of exchanging Christmas presents, she said, "George and I do not do presents. We have everything we want in life. If we don't have something and one feels they need it, one gets it. I need a lot of clothes, so I buy them. Maybe I could say George gave me this or that. He gave me every darn thing I have. But I don't have to ask for it. Don't feel sorry that we don't exchange presents."

After George lost his reelection bid in 1992, she quipped, "He may not be able to keep a job, but he's certainly never boring."

On the secret of the longevity of their marriage, Barbara revealed who their role models were. "We also had wonderful parents who loved each other. That was a great gift."

"Can you imagine a man who would jump out of two perfectly good airplanes?...My husband, George, makes me laugh and has a wonderful sense of adventure," she said about the parachute jumps George always took. About his planned parachute jump on his eightieth birthday, she pointed out that "I've already told him that no matter which way it goes, this is his last jump."

The journalist Diane Sawyer asked about her husband's appearance once: "Is he still the handsomest man you've ever seen?"

Barbara responded, "Yes, uh-huh, uh-huh. I'm—my eyesight's getting bad though."

"You ask [our children] and they would tell you that [George's] worst side was he listened to every side of every argument and never gave them advice, let them think it out for themselves. They might say it was his most frustrating habit, only because a couple of times they really wanted advice, they really wanted him to say, 'I think you ought to do this.'"

"Some people are motivated by money, some people by power, and some people by public service. I put George in that latter category. He felt he'd made enough money for us to live and so he stopped working. He had no great ambitions to make a lot of money. I don't think you'd ever put George down as power mad. It's just public service."

Barbara Bush

"When I go back and read what I've written, I realize how much I've enjoyed my life."

First Mom

First Ladies

Being a First Lady had its perks. "You get to meet the best of everything, the best musicians, the best artists, the best—you get to meet heads of state, and I don't care if they're good or bad, they have to be the best to be that, even temporarily maybe."

"The wife of the president of the United States is probably the most spoiled woman in the world. You'd have to be awfully spoiled if you lived the life we live and wished for something else."

Barbara once wrote about her role as First Lady: "I'm not sure the American people like the spouse to be too front and center."

"[The president] doesn't need a wife to stir up more controversy for him."

On her popularity as a First Lady, she remarked, "I'm just a nice, fat grandmother who doesn't threaten anyone."

When her husband decided to run for president, Roger Ailes, his campaign media adviser, suggested that Barbara spruce herself up. "I'll do anything you want, but I won't dye my hair, change my wardrobe, or lose weight."

On being constantly asked during her husband's presidential campaign what kind of First Lady she would make, she complained, "I wish they'd quit asking me that."

"The honeymoon is still on," Barbara admitted during her early days as First Lady. "I'm not really sure I am the First Lady of the land, but I like being married to the president."

For her second international trip as First Lady, she decided to pack a lot more clothes than for the first trip. "I forgot that of course you can't just throw on

something and get on an airplane and then change
your clothes on the plane. You've got to be seen
getting on and off."

On getting together with other First Ladies,
Barbara said, "They're heroines to me. We rarely get
together except for a library opening or a funeral."

Barbara Bush once shared her thoughts on Eleanor
Roosevelt with Larry King on his TV program *Larry
King Live.*

LARRY KING: Where did you see the role—Eleanor
Roosevelt, whom I was fortunate enough to interview
before she died, said that she thought it was the role of
the good First Lady to give her husband her input.

BARBARA BUSH: That's right.

LARRY: Whether he used it or not is his call.

BARBARA: And she did, and he couldn't get out, but
she got out; and she was the most visible First Lady.
She wrote for money—a column.

LARRY: My Day.

BARBARA: That's right. I mean, times are different,
but she was certainly the forerunner of the, you

know, the twenty-first-century wife.

When Barbara met a black dog who was given a new name in honor of her visit to a Seattle child-care center, she learned of its name: Eleanor Roosevelt Kennedy Bush. Her response was: "Are her politics changing?" She paused. "Not that it matters, of course."

When asked during the 1992 campaign where she'd place herself between Bess Truman on one side and Eleanor Roosevelt on the other, she said "I always thought Bess Truman was terrific. I got ridiculed for that once, but she was a great wife. So was Eleanor Roosevelt....I think I'm half Eleanor, half Bess. I think I go out and do a lot of things. I do lots of traveling and a lot of programs....I really stay out of government business if I possibly can."

When the journalist Liz Smith asked her which First Lady she felt herself to be most like, Barbara said, "I don't think you have to be 'like' anyone. Why don't you ask me which First Ladies I liked? I liked them all, but I love Lady Bird Johnson—she hit a spark with me. When we got to Washington, she was the only First Lady I'd ever met, and she opened her doors to us. She is the most gracious, warm person."

Larry King asked Barbara once about her feelings about other First Ladies.

LARRY KING: The First Ladies are kind of like a union, aren't you?

BARBARA BUSH: Well, I guess so. We're the only people in America who ever shared that job, I guess.

LARRY: And there's a camaraderie, isn't there? A kind of a...

BARBARA: Yes. There's a genteelness about it.

LARRY: You liked Pat Nixon a great deal.

BARBARA: I loved Pat Nixon very, very much.

LARRY: Probably the least known of all.

BARBARA: That's right, but she certainly wasn't to the congressional wives of—I was one of those at that time. And she just was a great lady. And you know, her children are fabulous. And that, I mean—that's something, too.

LARRY: And Jackie Kennedy.

BARBARA: I loved her. I didn't know her and I was,

I think, the only First Lady who didn't sort of write something about her. But I didn't because I thought it would be presumptuous; but that didn't mean I didn't admire her enormously.

Which First Ladies made for better role models? "The ones I respected the most are the ones who did their own thing. I wish you wouldn't say Eleanor. I grew up in a household that really detested her. She just irritated my mother. I admire Pat Nixon for some reasons, Betty Ford for some reasons. Mrs. Nixon was one of the most courageous, loyal women I've ever known. She was the most down-to-earth. A lovely lady. And Betty Ford, she's almost now more than then. I admire her enormously. She's in great pain. She goes around the country working for arthritis, working for drug abuse problems."

"I think Mrs. [Rosalynn] Carter has to be the bravest woman in the world to take herself to Detroit and campaign for her husband. I believe in being supportive to your husband—and she must love him a bunch—but I'd have been scared to death if that had

Barbara Bush

been George Bush and I had to go to a city where they had forty percent unemployment with minorities and stand up and tell them my husband had been good and things were getting better. There's nothing wrong with being a strong, supportive wife—if you have a strong husband. I think she missed on that. I think I'm strong. It's not a quality I would have aimed for, but I think I am."

Comparing her style of influence on the White House to that of Nancy Reagan—who often used her husband's friends and aides to bear down on him— she said, "We do things differently. I have always been able to go through George.

"If I thought something was hurting George, I would certainly say to him, 'George, I think Jane Smith is doing you a disservice.' I wouldn't say 'Fire her' or 'Fire him.' That's not really the way we work. We have a good marriage. One reason it's good, maybe, is I don't fool around with his office and he doesn't fool around with my household."

On her relationship with Nancy Reagan while

being Second Lady, Barbara said, "I was always grateful that Nancy and I could be very good friends and didn't have to do stuff together all the time. I don't mean that quite the way it sounds. I mean, I had interests of my own that I wanted to do, so I didn't feel I had to run around and be a lady-in-waiting. It was just a nice feeling."

She realized early on that she and Nancy Reagan weren't going to be close when the Reagans moved into the White House. "We're not going to be able to have hobbies together. I jog and she rides; she probably would rather die than jog and I put riding up to the top of my rather-die list."

She told the TV journalist Cokie Roberts once while she was Second Lady: "For instance, look at the White House. Two hundred people have a pass to the White House. I remember sitting in this very house, talking to Nancy Reagan one day, and I said to her, 'You know, this morning I was working at my desk, and I suddenly thought, "I'm going to go right outside and take a walk." Then I thought of you;

you can't just walk outside and take a walk!' Those
beautiful eyes of hers were sort of misty...It would
be very hard to be First Lady. It's hard enough to be
Second. But that's one of the sacrifices you have to
make. Having said that, there are so many pluses,
I mean, you are living in history. You have an
opportunity to a lot of good things, and you have to
sacrifice something."

Barbara loved living at the vice presidential
mansion. "I feel so lucky being here. I think how
awful it must be for Nancy Reagan not being able to
walk around the lawn [at the White House], having
strangers wandering through the downstairs rooms
all morning."

She was able to poke fun at her status as Second
Lady while Nancy Reagan was living in the White
House. Nancy was a petite size three, often dressed
in designer outfits and Harry Winston jewels. And
there was Barbara herself, who was a size fourteen,
and who often wore fake pearls and sensible shoes.

On being constantly compared to Nancy Reagan, she admitted, "I hate it, because first of all, I lose on that particular comparison. But she and I are not alike and you can't compare apples and oranges, or whatever. And that doesn't take away from my enormous respect for her, and the job she's doing. So I hate that, the comparisons I read.

"Of course I'm not going to be the same. She's a perfectionist and I'm not. Our lifestyles are very, very different. Would I like to be like her? You bet. But there's no chance of that...she has a flair that I'll never have."

At a charity roast in Washington, D.C., she admitted this about Nancy: "As you know, we have a lot in common. She adores her husband; I adore mine. She fights drugs; I fight illiteracy. She wears a size three—so's my leg."

On Kitty Dukakis, the wife of the Democratic candidate for the presidency in 1988, she admitted, "I'd love to look like her if you want to know the truth."

Barbara Bush

After giving Hillary Rodham Clinton a tour of the White House, Barbara told her while being surrounded by members of the press: "I know a lot of wonderful men married to pills, and I know a lot of pills married to wonderful women. So one shouldn't judge that way."

On whether her standing as a First Lady would be compared to Hillary Clinton's, she said in 1992: "I think you don't get the report card...until the four years are over, and I'd be interested to know who accomplishes the most."

On Hillary Clinton: "She certainly is a very good lawyer. Everybody does things differently and she's considerably younger, so I wouldn't be spending hours—though I have a lot of friends who are younger—but it's very hard to say do you like someone who's running against your husband and cutting him to pieces. I'm not gonna stand around and say I love her, but I don't dislike her, and I felt very sorry for her in the beginning, because this is not a game you go into without being touched and I think she got touched quite a lot."

Comparing herself to Hillary Clinton, she cracked, "Yes, we're both young and good-looking."

"The May [1995] issue of *Outlaw Biker* magazine named me 'Biker Babe of the Century' and said that I was a 'classy broad.' As this magazine usually features topless and tattooed women, and bikers in black leather, I really was honored. Referring to Desert Storm, they also had a line in there about 'Babs' old man who kicked a little butt in the White House.' Definitely a very fine honor!"

Regarding Hillary Clinton's run for the United States Senate from New York, Barbara said, "I think that's fine. Let her do what she wants, and when she loses, I think she'll feel very badly." (Senator Clinton went on to win the New York senatorial election by a wide margin.)

"I got so excited when George [W.] was elected governor [of Texas]. I got to thinking maybe I could

run. I'm thinking of New Jersey, but I was born in
New York. Had I chosen it, I think, I'd be the only native running there."

Asked whether she gave any advice to Laura Bush, she responded, "No, I really didn't have to, I think she's so much smarter than I am. But she was there [during the 1992 campaign for reelection], so she knows about campaigning."

Barbara Bush

The
White House

After being given a personal tour by Nancy Reagan of the family quarters upstairs at the White House, she enthused: "It's the most beautiful house I've ever seen. I'm not going to change a thing."

While showing off the White House to journalists, she gushed a bit. "Everything glistens. It's so much more beautiful than I thought. Everything is beautiful in the White House. Honestly. The food is the most beautiful food you've ever laid your eyes on. Today I had lunch off of Wilson's plates, sometimes I have lunch off of Lincoln's plates, or Grover Cleveland's."

When asked about the worst part of being in the White House, she said, "The day you become president, for the rest of your life you give up privacy. And that was an enormous shock to me."

On her early days in the White House she said, "It's much more fun than I thought it would be."

When Barbara found out that the White House had a washer and dryer on the premises, she and Paola Rendon, the housekeeper for the Bush family for thirty years, were ecstatic. "There are three of each. She'll just have those running all the time. I said to Paola, 'You're going to be in heaven.'"

When she moved into the White House, she took out Nancy Reagan's hair dryers to make room for her family's five dozen scrapbooks, which she called "the essence of our life."

"[Nancy Reagan] did advise me not to have my children live in the White House—for whatever that's worth. I told her I hadn't invited them."

Even though she was living in the White House, she feared being isolated. "I'm working on a theory. I'm going to go out so much that you're going to be saying, 'Ho-hum, there's Mrs. Bush out again.' I'm going to go to museums. I'm going to walk. I'm going to go out with friends. I'm just going to do things, because I think there's a danger in...I mean, look how pretty it is; who would ever want to leave it? But I think it's very important to get out."

But later she said, "The world comes to you. I mean, we're not as isolated as you might think. We've seen thousands of people."

When Barbara became First Lady, she worried about the kinds of meals she and her guests would be served at the White House, as they might affect her weight problem. But she noticed that the portions served by waiters were quite small. "Why aren't they feeding us?"

As it turned out, Nancy Reagan had instructed the chefs to serve such tiny portions. Barbara decided not to change this policy, asking for seconds and thirds instead.

Barbara once pointed out that the Lincoln Sitting Room was where Richard Nixon prayed with Henry Kissinger two days before he finally resigned during the Watergate era. "There is the little sitting room that's only notable because supposedly, remember, when President Nixon and Kissinger went in—it had a fire in the fireplace and air-conditioning in July."

On the only signed and dated copy of the Gettysburg Address displayed in one corner of the historic Lincoln Bedroom, she said, "It's not a thing of great beauty but pretty exciting."

When she showed the burn marks on the Truman Balcony overlooking the South Lawn to Queen Elizabeth, she told her, "This is where the British tried to burn down the White House."
The queen didn't seem too pleased.

After her husband told the country he enjoyed pork rinds, Barbara admitted that she had no intention of serving them at the White House even though they kept getting caseloads of them. "I wish George had never said he liked them."

After the Persian Gulf War ended, the White House

was reopened to tourists. "I missed the tourists. I missed having them come through the house. And I felt...I think the house missed them too."

When asked whether she'd ever warned George W. and Laura Bush about what it was like to live in the White House, she said: "They know exactly what's in front of them. And the fact that they chose to give up privacy, I think, is a wonderful thing. But there are many more pluses than minuses. I mean, we still live in a fishbowl. That's sort of the disappointing thing about leaving the White House—you don't leave behind the sightseers....But the pluses are so much more than the minuses. The fact that you can do good for people and you can help people, and that you know the best of everything in our country and our world."

People and Places

O n meeting various world leaders while accompanying her husband to sixty-eight countries, she said, "Not that they know me, but I know them."

"One morning...I turned on the television and suddenly realized that, with the exception of [Yasser] Arafat, I knew every single person personally that I had seen on the tube during that hour. That's the life that George Bush has given me. Amazing life. Lucky, lucky me."

In Toronto for a concert, Barbara said, "We love Canadians. That's one thing my husband sent me off with. He said: 'You're going to go up there and tell them how much we love and respect Canada.'"

Her directness didn't always translate so well in other countries. On a visit with her husband to

108   Tokyo, she sat next to Japan's late emperor Hirohito at a luncheon. While she lavished compliments on her surroundings and the decor of the imperial palace, its seeming newness puzzled her. "Was the former palace so old, it crumbled?" "No," replied Hirohito stiffly. "I'm afraid that you bombed it."

Of a picture that showed Emperor Hirohito standing with George and Barbara, she was fond of quipping, "Papa Bear, Mama Bear, and Baby Bear."

When she went to Africa in 1985, she visited areas struck by famine. It was a very emotional trip for her, as she met a great many emaciated children. She noticed that many starving babies had their heads completely shaved except for one row of hair. "They told us they had that so God can reach down and pull them up to heaven."

Even though Barbara had been warned not to eat salads or any uncooked foods while on her Africa trip, she said, "This is their country, and they're serving salad, so I'm going to eat it."

Barbara Bush

In Ghana she had to watch a man bite off the head of a chicken. "I made up my mind that no matter what he did, I wouldn't react. And I didn't react. But people around me were dropping like flies."

She shared her impressions of Saudi women: "I was fascinated, even in the change since we were there ten years ago. They know it's important to educate women; they say when you educate the woman, you educate the family. Many of the four hundred or so women I talked to had not only M.A.'s but had Ph.D.'s or were pediatricians or university presidents. I was very encouraged. I saw quite a few American women there who were very much at home. When in Rome, do as the Romans do."

Barbara said that Mikhail Gorbachev "whispered, 'Barbara, I want to take you to all the nightclubs the next time you're in Russia.'" Her response? "I have been to Moscow before, but I have only been to funerals, so anything is up."

She wrote a brief obituary about her friend Raisa

Gorbachev for *Time* magazine. Part of it read: "When I met Raisa Gorbachev in 1987, the cold war still divided our countries, but it did not prevent us from becoming good friends. It was tough at first. We came from different cultures. Raisa passionately believed in communism and was not afraid to defend it.

"But while our husbands were trying to resolve serious differences, Raisa and I discovered we were much alike. We talked about our children, how difficult it could be to live a public life, and of course we talked about our husbands. We both just happened to be crazy about the men we married."

After a dinner with Prince Charles at the vice-presidential mansion, she said that having him as a dinner companion was "like sitting next to one of my four sons only he's better dressed and more polite."

On Diana, the Princess of Wales, she reflected, "I didn't think I'd like the little princess from England. But Diana is the most outgoing lady. I took her to a hospice. She sat on the beds of people who were in the last two weeks of life, held their hands, and asked how they felt. They glowed. She said, 'How are you being helped? Is the program working? Are you in any pain? Does your medication help?' And these people told her."

Shortly after her husband was chosen by Ronald Reagan as his running mate, Barbara admitted, "I'm assuming everybody knows that I thought George would be the best qualified person for president. I haven't changed on that, but I'm thrilled that if it couldn't be George, it's Governor Reagan. And I'm surprised about that, but I'm very truthful about that."

She called Ronald Reagan "the kindest man, next to George Bush, I ever knew."

"In April [1996], during a trip to Los Angeles, we went by to see Ronald Reagan at his office. This was so very sad. He looked wonderful, and it was very clear that he had absolutely no idea who we were. It really made George very unhappy as he respected and loved Ron very much. He still was innately polite, and yet one got the feeling that he was faking.

First Mom

We didn't stay very long, and as we left, George told him that we just wanted to say hello, that we missed him, and loved him. He answered something like, 'You must drop in anytime.' He looked so confused, like he knew he should have remembered us or something. That was the last time I saw Ron. I won't remember the man we saw that day. I will remember that gentle, wise, decent, warm, funny man."

When Geraldine Ferraro was running for vice president in 1984, Barbara Bush told a reporter how she felt about Ms. Ferraro: "Four-million-dollar—I can't say it, but it rhymes with 'rich.'"

Afterward, she opted for an immediate apology and told reporters: "The poet laureate has retired."

She revealed her observations about Jesse Jackson: "A big man who fills a room. He must be a chore for the Democrats. He has his own agenda and has never missed a funeral, a strike, or a march."

"There's no question that [the 1988 Democratic candidate for the presidency] Mike Dukakis is a

fabulous debater. You got to have card sense, too, in
life. I know a lot of people who got all A's in school
but couldn't cope with life. I'm not saying that Mike
Dukakis is that, because he certainly is one of two
people seeking the highest job in the land and
I think he's very bright. And being one of two is
something."

On Dan Quayle, the vice presidential nominee on
her husband's ticket for the presidency, Barbara said,
"I think he's better qualified to be vice president
than [the Democrat candidate] Mike Dukakis is
to be president. I really feel that way. You never
know until someone steps up to the bat how they're
going to hit, and I think you're going to find he is
exceptional."

On Anita Hill's allegations of sexual harassment
against the Supreme Court nominee Clarence
Thomas, she said, "I don't believe the allegations
against him. I know him to be a superb, superior
individual."

On whether she watched the Democratic convention of 1992 in which the presidential nominee Al Gore brought out his thirteen-year-old son, who'd survived an automobile accident, as proof of spirtual and family values, she said, "I did not watch that convention. I didn't. I am certainly not a sadist...what's that word? Masochist? I'm not that, that's for darn sure. But of course I know about Al Gore's son—the president was very involved in that; he wrote the boy, had him come to the White House, and had pictures taken afterward....Was Gore exploitative, manipulative? That's their business, I have no opinion on that. Everybody has to do their own—his or her own—thing. I might judge, but I'm not going to cast stones. I might in my heart say I wouldn't have done that—but, no. I don't think there's a rule for what's good taste or bad taste, I think that's up to what he feels in his heart. And what the little kid feels. And I didn't see the convention anyway."

On the Monica Lewinsky scandal that was starting to brew around President Clinton, Barbara Bush was quite succinct: "Clinton lied. A man might forget where he parks or where he lives, but he never forgets oral sex, no matter how bad it is."

When she learned that Pat Buchanan was leaving the Republican party for a third party, she said: "I'm sorry he left. He's like a whiny child who picks up his marbles and leaves."

Barbara made a stab at Senator John McCain and the national news media once, saying his campaign has been boosted by reporters looking to generate excitement in the presidential race. "Without sounding like I'm whining, I feel he's [McCain] had enormous help from the press, because he's become sort of a star figure with them," she said in an interview with *The Arizona Republic.* "I think they wanted a race, and I think they wanted a Bradley–Gore race too."

Reading

O n why she chose literacy as her leading cause: "I knew George was going to run for high office and I'd always volunteered in hospitals. And I thought about it and thought, I ought to pick a project that will help the most people possible and probably not cost too much more government money and certainly not be controversial. I mean, why pick a cause that's going to cause trouble always in the family. But having said that, when I jogged and thought, now I worry about pregnant teenagers—and I do worry about that—and I worry about high school dropouts and I worry about a ton of things that all of us worry about. We didn't have AIDS then, and we really didn't have homelessness. But I worry about all those things—the environment, everything. It suddenly occurred to me, if more people could read and write and comprehend, everything would be better."

On her childhood full of reading, she said, "My father was in the publishing business [Marvin Pierce was president of the company that published *McCall's* and *Redbook*] and my first memories are of my mother and father sitting after dinner, reading."

"I really waited monthly for the next installment of those things [magazines that featured serial stories]. And when I got to boarding school, they told me that was trash reading. And I told my dad, 'You can't send me those magazines anymore, it's trash reading.' He said, 'Look, you tell them that trash is sending you to school.'"

"I was lucky to have parents who took me to the library and could afford to buy me books."

"Libraries are extraordinarily different from what they used to be when I would walk down to the Rye library and get my books every Saturday morning. Today everything's on a computer, they have all sorts of places where you can learn, it's almost like a tiny little community college. And there's storybook time

Barbara Bush

for the children—that alone is worth the whole library, because you get children coming in, being read to, you get the mothers used to reading to their children."

"Our young people need to know that reading is a joy as well as the most essential of skills, and that libraries are inviting, accessible places dedicated to the joy of reading."

First Mom

"Libraries and librarians have definitely changed my life—and the lives of countless other Americans.... They deserve the support and patronage of every single one of us who values education."

"All of a sudden what you're seeing now is all the literacy programs getting together and working through unemployment and driver's license agencies and libraries and suddenly they're doing a much better job. The government is doing a lot of networking, so when someone is talking about job training, they're also talking about education. They're not competing, but working together."

"I've visited a lot of Project Head Starts and they're wonderful. But they really aren't as wonderful as they could be, because, in many cases, they're not working with the mothers and fathers. That's one thing that sort of got me. I mean, I could have had just a Barbara Bush Foundation for Literacy but in the last three or four years it has come to me that the family is what makes the difference. The home is the child's first school. The parent is the child's first teacher. Reading is the child's first subject."

Barbara Bush

"Please remember to read to your children and grandchildren. It's important to instill in them early an urge to read," she said. "And don't forget to turn off the TV."

"If we can read and write, we can learn; if we can learn, we can get a job and support ourselves and our families. We'd be less tempted to turn to drugs, alcohol, or crime, or to drop out of school, or get pregnant before we're ready. We'll have pride and be able to enjoy the very best in life—including a good book or bedtime stories with our children."

After reading the Christmas story from the Bible to a group of children with their mothers, she announced, "This is a good story, so good it lasted almost two thousand years."

"Just keep in mind that each of you has a special gift to give—the gift of reading," she once said. "Few gifts are more precious. No other gift strengthens the mind and nourishes the soul like reading does. No other gift gives rise to our dreams like literacy."

First Mom

"I'll bet you half the Americans out there have never read a book for fun."

"Kids who don't see their parents reading are less likely to do so themselves."

"If you know how to read," she said, "find someone who can't. If you have a hammer, find a nail."

She began her speech at a major fund-raiser designed to support the literacy cause in which a variety of writers would read from their work: "Welcome to this year's Celebration of Reading. I can hardly believe it, but this is our seventh year. We see so many familiar faces coming from year to year that we're beginning to think that you even maybe enjoy the evening, or that you're gluttons for punishment."

"I read in the paper that Mrs. Bush reads a book a day—for seven days I read a cheap little novel a day, only seven days—but now I've gone down in history as the world's biggest nut, who never reads the newspapers, never listens to television, and reads a book a day."

Barbara Bush

"If some illiterates make it, it's because they're considerably smarter than the rest of us, because they've had to fake it so, and have had to really use all sorts of other talents....But there are so many of them who went right through college, and that is so disgraceful, it's just embarrassing. But it's also embarrassing when we let a little kid go through kindergarten, first, second, third grade, who doesn't know how to read, and he goes through life bearing this guilt burden, and it's not his fault."

In an op-ed piece she wrote on literacy for *The Washington Post* in 1984, she said, "They can't read signs in a department store. They don't know what the directions on a medicine bottle say. They can't look in the want ads for a job or fill out a job application form. The personal cost to these people is very high. They suffer the frustration of constant helplessness and the continuing fear of being found out and humiliated."

Barbara suggested to *Publishers Weekly* that the publishing industry help her crusade against illiteracy. "I think they ought to be having a little look-see at what they have in their own offices. Because it's fantastic, the number of newspapers and publishing businesses that have found that they, too, harbor some very bright, very smart illiterates."

She enthused over First Lady Laura Bush's literacy campaign: "That daughter-in-law of mine has it right: We have to educate the world and we can only start at home."

"Both George and I go to sleep reading every night."

Barbara Bush's Family Reading Tips

1. Establish a routine for reading aloud.
2. Make reading together a special time.
3. Try these simple ways to enrich reading aloud with your children:
   a. Move your finger under the words as you read.
   b. Let your child help turn the pages.
   c. Take turns reading words, sentences, or pages.

Barbara Bush

d. Pause and ask open-ended questions such as "How would you feel if you were that person?" or "What do you think might happen next?"

e. Look at the illustrations and talk about them.

f. Change your voice as you read different characters' words. Let your child make up voices.

g. Keep stories alive by acting them out.

4. Ask others who take care of your children to read aloud.

5. Visit the library regularly.

6. Let your children see you reading.

7. Read all kinds of things together.

8. Fill your home with opportunities for reading.

9. Keep reading aloud even after your children learn to read.

On the Issues

Whenever she is asked about political issues of the day, her answer is always: "I'm not an elected official."

"I share with George the information I gather about the homeless. In fact, he teases me when I take soap and shampoo from the hotels to send to women's shelters. For instance, when we stay in a hotel, we are given five bars of soap. George and I share one, and I send the other four to the shelters so each woman can have her own soap."

"I'm not [against people wearing fur]. I probably wouldn't myself, but I'm not opposed to people wearing it. I'm not going to sit in judgment of what people wear. So often people who are critical of that do wear shoes, sit on leather chairs. I'm against cruelty to animals. But it's not an issue with me."

On Tipper Gore's stance against explicitness in contemporary music's lyrics, which led to the labeling of albums with violent and obscenely sexual images, she said, "I'd like to see Tipper Gore stand up and hang in against it. The things they're talking about are so bad, you can't believe them. That song about policemen is unspeakable. Disgusting. Tipper Gore was right, and I don't think she ought to back off...Will she be persuaded to? Well, we'll see; I don't know."

Barbara was once featured in a series of television and radio commercials designed to convince voters to reject the initiatives to legalize marijuana as "medicine."

"Hello. I'm Barbara Bush. Some of the most rewarding experiences of my life have come from working with children. As parents and grandparents, George and I have learned firsthand the joys and challenges of raising a family in today's world. That is why I would like to speak with you about an issue of great concern to us both. Over the past several years, there has been a dangerous trend of drug use by young people in our country. More and more are experimenting with illegal drugs and more are using drugs on a regular basis. That is why we are concerned about efforts to legalize marijuana and other illegal substances. Now is not the time to send a message to our young people that marijuana is medicine. It is not. It is a dangerous, illegal drug."

"You know George has always been against gun control. Well, I have always been for gun control. For thirty-five years I have been for gun control. Now, this should give you two deep insights on the situation. The first insight is what great influence I have on George Bush. And the second is how George feels about gun control...It's just a thing with me, how I feel about gun control. I just don't feel it's any big deal to register a gun."

She once opined that AK-47 assault weapons should be illegal. "They should be—absolutely."

"I myself do not own a gun. I'm afraid of them. I'm too afraid I'd shoot the wrong person."

First Mom

"Abortion, number one, is not a major item with me—it's not a top priority with me. But, you know, I think the person who has the courage to run for the office is the one you should hear, not the wife or the husband. Having said that, of course I told George how I felt; but, you know, when you're as close to your husband as I am to mine—he knew how I felt; I'd told him. And I knew how he felt and I never questioned the sincerity of his beliefs."

"I'm not being outspoken on pro or con abortion. I'm saying abortion should not be in there [the Republican convention platform], either pro or con. I mean, I have friends who are pro-Bush, pro-choice. I have friends who are pro-life, pro-Bush. That's right. I mean, that's the way it should be, I think...And fine, you're pro-choice. I understand that. And great if you're pro-life. I understand that too. And I know that you can argue yourself blue in the face and you're not going to change each other's mind. And it's a waste of your time and my time to try to change minds. People feel very strongly both ways."

Barbara Bush

When asked if she'd support one of her children having an abortion, Barbara said, "If my child broke a law, which this would not be breaking, but if my child broke a law, that doesn't mean I condone it. But I would certainly put my arms around her and hug her and love her and care for her. And I believe George said he would counsel the child. But, you know, you can't pin a child down and say you can't have an abortion; that's against the law."

While talking about abortion with Larry King on television, she said, "I think the issue is that we ought to tell children that sex is death. It is. Promiscuous sex is death. They shouldn't be doing that; we ought to be telling these wonderful young women there's a great deal of life out there for you if you finish school, if you get a job, then you can have a family. But you just shouldn't be having promiscuous sex. It just ruins your life."

"No one likes abortion. It's the last resort. It's not birth control."

The Gulf War

When her grandchildren asked her about the Persian Gulf War, she said, "I reminded them that a perfectly peaceful country was sitting there and another country invaded it and we cannot have that."

She felt deeply for the American soldiers stuck in the desert heat. "I hate it because families are being broken up. I feel just like any other mother would. How do you think George feels—that's what kills me—because he really feels each one of those [young soldiers] are his."

"Someone on the *Nassau* passed me a letter saying, 'Don't forget our wives, who are so courageous at home.' He wrote, 'They're really the brave ones'—his wife and four children.

"And he said, 'You and the president keep them in your prayers.' I thought that was so sweet. We do pray every night."

She shared her observations on how the troops treated her on her Thanksgiving visit. "I was amazed by how many cameras the troops had. They asked us to autograph everything—pictures of their babies, pictures of their dogs, their springer spaniels. They asked me to sign pictures of their wives, their hats, their coats, their Bibles."

She pulled back whenever she saw guns on the marines themselves. "I rarely hug guns."

The Bushes brought home a lot of souvenirs from the troops. "We were sort of tucking things in pockets. It was very moving. I have to confess, every time a helicopter took off, I felt like crying. It just—seemed so final."

About the horrific footage of the Persian Gulf War, she had this to say: "My kids aren't different than anyone else's. I just think parents should

Barbara Bush

monitor their children and just be sure that they're understanding what they're seeing so they're not getting terrible nightmares. I just think you ought to be careful of your children."

As for the fate of Saddam Hussein, she said: "I'd like to see him hung...if he were found guilty. I mean, we're talking about thousands and thousands of lives that have been tortured and...I'm sure you have all talked to people who came back from Kuwait. But it's just horrible, the stories they tell."

First Mom

She advised the wives and families of soldiers still based in Kuwait: "Keep life at home on an even keel. This relieves their worries about you and it helps ensure a wonderful homecoming for them. By tending to daily life, by making sure that the dentist appointments are kept and the mortgage payments get made, the homework gets done, Little League games get watched, you are doing the most essential service of all."

She revealed why she understood their emotional plight. "You know, many years ago, when our country was fighting another just war, I was a college girl in Massachusetts. But my heart was not in the classroom. At least, that's how I explained my grades to my parents then. My heart and thoughts were somewhere in the Pacific on the USS *Jacinto*, a converted light cruiser, with a wonderful young naval pilot to whom I happened to be engaged. So we do understand a little bit of what you've been through."

Barbara Bush

Barbara Bush
On Women

She once paid tribute to Florida's women: "You are making Florida a stronger, better state," she said. "If there were three wise women instead of three wise men, they would have asked for directions, arrived on time, helped deliver the baby, cleaned the stables, brought a casserole, cooked the casserole, and brought practical gifts. You all are wise women."

"I think many women, certainly of my generation, can run the world. And some of them have waited until their children have gone off and they've been grandparents and have taken on major projects for money."

While campaigning for her son George W., she predicted that the country would see a female president. "I fully expect to see a female president.

She'll be a Republican, of course, but I fully expect to see her, and I don't expect to live too many more years."

In 1984 she shared her thoughts on equality for women: "I don't think men and women should have children and not take responsibility. Men are going to have to take a lot more responsibility. They will have to do more as their share. But women are also going to have to learn that they have to have priorities, that they have to make choices, and that they can't have everything. You can't, in my opinion, be a bank president and a full-time mother."

"I want equal rights for women, men, everybody. Equal rights for every American. Equal pay for equal work."

"I've been brought up in a family where if your husband wanted to do something, you'd do it, and gladly. I still think there's nothing wrong with that. I would say the same if a wife wanted to do something very badly. Her husband should do the same."

Barbara Bush

"I'm not critical [of women who make the dual choice of career and motherhood]. I have daughters [in-law] who work. I don't think it's easy."

On whether she—or George Bush—would try to bridge the gender gap, she said, "I don't know. I'm certainly going to try, but I think he'll do it himself. I'm really surprised, because most women I think are interested in the same things George is interested in: a good education for their children, and their husbands and their children and themselves having jobs and being able to get into the system. I use as an example—and it's not a great example because we're not the average family—but before the Reagan—Bush administration, we had four children who were not in the system. That is, they weren't beginning to buy a house, starting to get going on the ground floor. Now, because interest rates are down, five of them are buying houses. Not the biggest houses in the world, but they're buying them and that puts them in the system; that makes them part of the American dream."

On whether women should fight in combat, she said, "The average man is better at throwing a hand grenade. I myself am very athletic, but I have never been able to throw a ball as far as a man."

On the negative effects of the women's liberation movement, she said that today's women who choose to be stay-at-home moms get "a down-in-the-dumps feeling about themselves, even though in their hearts they know they really want to spend their time with their children. They suddenly see that other women are out, smartly dressed, mixing with exciting people. They think, 'Everybody else is having fun and I'm sitting home, talking to four-year-olds.'"

Barbara Bush

Children and Family

"I think the way to judge a mother is by her children."

"I always recommend to parents that they get their children to write in diaries, and then I worry: What if the parents read them? That's wrong. If you tell a child to write what he feels and then you look at it, it's unfair. Whatever it is, you don't need to know it."

According to the columnist Peggy Noonan, she saw how shocked Nancy Reagan was to learn that her son Ron Reagan remarked in an interview that the only accomplishment George W. had to his name was to stop drinking, and called Barbara to apologize. This happened during the presidential race of 2000. Her response was: "Oh, Nancy, don't give it a thought. We can't control our children."

She reflected on their early days of raising a family in Midland, Texas. "We both knew that if we got into trouble, someone would help us. And so to say we knew what it was like to be poor is ridiculous. For us, it was a challenge and exciting and we'd rather have died than asked. But it's very easy to say when you know you've got a mother and father—in fact, two—who would help...that's very different."

"Although we have the same problems that any large family would have, we are blessed to be surrounded by love and caring. If ever again a minister asks those of us who have perfect families to please raise their hands, mine will go up in a minute."

Taking care of her children in Texas was un-forgettable. "This was a period, for me, of long days and short years; of diapers, runny noses, earaches, more Little League games than you could believe possible, tonsils, and those unscheduled races to the hospital emergency room; Sunday school and church; of hours of urging homework, short, chubby arms around your neck and sticky kisses; and experiencing bumpy moments—not many, but few—of feeling that I'd never, ever be able to have fun again; and coping with the feeling that George Bush, in his excitement of starting a small company and traveling around the world, was having a lot of fun."

"My children have had only minor problems. They haven't had any real problems. And don't forget. I'm right there with them every step of the way....They're all wonderful kids. We've always been very conceited about how wonderful our family is."

"It's hard on you, but you have to put your children first. And I think your boss has to accommodate a little bit. I mean, if you need to go to school to see your child in a school situation, [the employer] should make accommodations for it. You'll have to make it up, but that's just a fact of life."

"Somehow or other, it made George and me feel that the life we had chosen was not so bad after all for the children. All of our children have made a lot of sacrifices and we couldn't help but wonder if they felt they would have been much luckier if they hadn't been in politics."

"Long ago I decided that in life I had to have priorities. I put my husband and children at the top of my list. That's a choice that I never regretted."

As for whether her kids were supported by inherited money, she said, "We haven't died yet! But no, they've never had any money from us. We did send them to college. But they worked every summer."

"We have the five most honest, decent children, who have sacrificed enormously, business-wise and everything else, to support their father because they think he's wonderful. And they are the most decent, honest people I know. They're the best parents, the best citizens, the most giving children and—you bet, I mean, I could go to fisticuffs over my children."

"I called George one day when the boys were small, and said, 'Your son just hit a ball through the neighbor's upstairs window.' And he said, 'My gosh, what a great hit.' And then he said, 'Did you get the ball back?'"

"When I grew up, my father would say, 'Why didn't you get an A?' I'd be so excited with a B plus. I would say to my kids, 'B? Hooray, you passed.' There's this difference. My father expected quality; I expected to just get through. I think that's a mistake. I think it's been proven that if you expect a lot from children, you get it."

She often asked people not to send her cards and letters in honor of Mother's Day. "Please don't write me. I have children of my own. I'm not your mother."

"I read that the Kennedy family sat around and talked about history," she said. "We didn't. We sat around and talked about friends. Just the things you all talked about. I'd love to come up with some brilliant something, but we didn't."

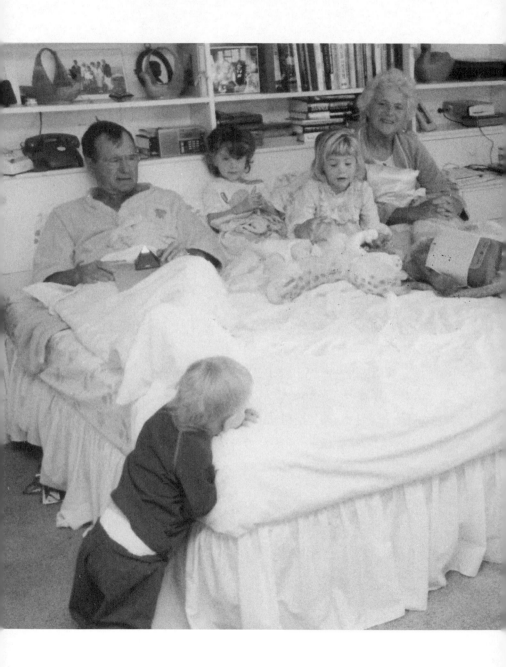

Barbara Bush

First Mom

"I think there's honestly a yearning for old-fashioned warmth and coziness and family, and people who aren't afraid to say they love each other. People like the fact that I love my children, and love and adore my husband. People come through receiving lines and sort of whisper, 'Can I hug you? Thanks for bringing family back.' They really say that. It's as though we've forgotten how to be families, how to be supportive of each other. I think people are yearning for that."

"I sense that young people are beginning to think in terms of extended family again. The extended families may not even be related. They may be neighbors, friends. People are saying, 'What affects me affects my neighbors.' When problems arise—crime, drugs, bad schools—each person says, 'This isn't good. I have to do something about it.'"

Once a Bush family outing somehow managed to pass by a nude beach. She remarked, "All people named Bush kept their clothes on, and have at least going back twenty-five years."

Barbara Bush

"I spanked. I didn't whip, but I spanked. Thank heaven no one knew it, or I'd be in jail."

The death of their daughter Robin from leukemia when she was not quite four left George and Barbara Bush with a lifelong compassion. She said, "Because of Robin, George and I love every living human more."

"Midland was wonderful" during the time when the Bushes had to deal with their daughter Robin's leukemia. "They all rallied around—the church and friends. It was an interesting time for me because some of my best friends, people I'd see all the time, really couldn't cope with Robin's sickness. Some of the people I knew only fairly well, like Betty Liedtke, whose husband was in business with George, never left my side. It was the most amazing thing. And when I brought Robin home, it was so scary because she'd hemorrhage and didn't eat and Betty was there every day with some wonderful food because if Robin didn't eat, we'd have to go back to New York [for additional treatment]."

On hearing the diagnosis of Robin's leukemia, she remarked, "[The doctor] gave us the best advice anyone could have given, which of course we didn't take. She said, 'Number one, don't tell anyone. Number two, don't treat her. You should take her home, make life as easy as possible for her, and in three weeks' time, she'll be gone.'"

On the impending death of their daughter Robin in 1953, she said, "George held me tight and wouldn't let me go. You know seventy percent of the people who lose children get divorced because one doesn't talk to the other. He did not allow that."

After Robin died, Barbara said, "The people who said to me, 'Time will cure,' I wanted to hit them right between the eyes. And someone once said to me, 'Well, look at it this way. It wasn't your firstborn, and it was a girl at that.' I almost fainted."

During her grieving period over her daughter Robin's death, she overheard her son George W. talking. "One day I heard Georgie tell a friend,

'I can't play today because I have to be with my mother—she's so unhappy.' That's when I realized you either pull together or you shatter."

On nearly losing their son Marvin to life-threatening ulcerative colitis, which required a colostomy, Barbara said, "We've realized there are worse things than losing an election. Marvin's very valuable to us. We knew it, but we didn't know how valuable. I just think that our fresh perspective had something to do with Marvin."

"No family is perfect, and no family is without pain and suffering. We lost a daughter [Robin]. We almost lost a son [Marvin]. And one child [Neil] struggled for years with a learning disability."

Sometimes she'd write to parents grieving over the loss of a child, saying, "If I could take your pain, I would. I'd like to put my arms around you.' Or sometimes I say, which I think is very important, 'You have other children and you've got to take care of them. Remember, they're hurting too.'"

"[George and I] are both of us so proud that our children have decided to serve their country. They're not children to you, but they're our children to us. It was very ugly in 1992 for our family. Not the loss, but the campaign was very ugly and yet these two young men weren't turned off because they want to serve their country."

"Thinking back on it, I was really surprised that George and Jeb wanted to have anything to do with politics after 1992. Both of them had worked hard in the campaign, and both of them had seen the tough, dirty side of politics—the lies and negative campaigning. Both of them saw and felt how much losing hurt. It does. As I recall, George W. asked us what we thought, and I told him that he should NOT run against the very popular Governor Ann Richards. I did not think he could win. His father was much wiser and offered no advice. To this day George W. teases me about that advice."

On her sons George W. and Jeb becoming politicians, she said, "I think it's fascinating they'd follow in their father's footsteps. Both were successful in business first. I don't mean that they're ragingly rich, but they did succeed. I think it's very important that you pay taxes and prove you can support your family, and that you're not supported by a government job alone."

"Our children, particularly [George and Jeb], have gotten into the fray, and they haven't sat back and complained about America. They've gotten out to do something to make it better for all Americans. And

First Mom

I'm very proud of that."

On the relationship between her sons George W. and Jeb, she remarked, "As adults, they support each other, love each other. When they were children growing up, I never believed they would grow up to be best friends."

Later on, Larry King asked Barbara Bush to share her feelings about her children's involvement with politics.

LARRY KING: How do you feel about two sons in politics, both running for governor of two huge states?

BARBARA BUSH: I think we're just—the country's lucky to have them. They're the two best-qualified, finest young men you've ever known.

LARRY: Were you surprised at either one of them entering the political ring?

BARBARA: Not really, because they'd worked so hard in their communities and in their parties for years. Both of them are pretty successful businessmen and have very strong families. And, I'll tell you, it touched both George and me because you might have thought they'd have been turned off after the ugly 1992. They love their father and he adores them. And for them to get into politics—and if you're listening, you bad boys—you made your dad and mom very happy.

At one of her campaign speeches, she lifted her eyebrows when she asked her audience: "Did you know one out of every eight Americans is governed by a Bush?"

"I am truly in awe [of Jeb, the governor of Florida]. This is the same son forty years ago I threatened with death and destruction if he didn't clean up his room. I find myself standing next to this amazing, smart man who happens to be governor and happens to be my son who shares my concerns. Life doesn't get better than that."

"Often when we watch Jeb give a speech, George and I are truly in awe."

First Mom

"[My husband] had a wonderful vision for America, but he had trouble articulating it. Honest to Pete, Jeb has a vision for the state of Florida and can tell you about it."

"Your homes, your streets, and your families are safer than ever before," Barbara proclaimed while stumping for Jeb on his reelection bid at a rally in Florida. "As proud as I am of all of these accomplishments, I am even more proud of the kind of man he is. You may not agree with all of the decisions that Jeb has made as governor, but you cannot help but agree that he has been a strong and decisive leader."

By way of explaining Jeb's success in obtaining a degree in Latin American studies and a Phi Beta Kappa key after just two and half years at the University of Texas, Barbara said that "he wanted to prove he was serious [about Columba Garnica Gallo, who eventually became his wife]. She thought he was a rich man's son and a playboy."

Barbara Bush

"The one thing you can count on, Jeb Bush will never let you down, and that's a mother's promise."

What convinced George W. Bush to run for president? According to *Time* magazine, it happened at a prayer service with his family in January 2000. "Pastor Mark Craig started preaching about duty, about how Moses tried to resist God's call, and the sacrifice that leadership requires. And as they sat there, Barbara Bush leaned over to the son who has always been most like her and said, 'He's talking to you, George.'"

"My husband's going to kill you. He's out of town, but he's coming home to kill you immediately" she once threatened the principal after telling her husband about how the principal had spanked W. for painting a mustache on his face in music class.

After being surprised by George W.'s performance on the basketball court at Andover, Coach DiClemente told his parents, "Well, your kid did a helluva job today."

Barbara shot back, "Well, what did you expect?"

"He's just run, you know, the—the state with the eleventh largest economy. Plus, he went to Yale and Harvard Business School. I mean, you just don't get into those schools and you don't do well as he did, certainly in the business school. I admit that Yale, he passed, and he was a leader at Yale. All of his classmates tell him that. So, I think you'll find George was maybe a slightly later bloomer than his father, but much earlier than his mother. That's the good news."

On George W.'s "new" presidential campaign, she gushed, "I'm crazy about him, and I loved watching him on TV yesterday. He's talking about all the things I think America is concerned about. I feel like we've done good with this boy."

"George W. has had a lot of fun in his life, we all know that," she said. "But his father and I were shocked to read he was an alcoholic. I don't believe that. But I

Barbara Bush

"I would have told you twenty years before that he was changing. Becoming disciplined. Those things come through a slow process, they don't happen all at once. But he is much more disciplined than I am. Every year he makes a New Year's resolution, and he keeps it. Last year he read the Bible all the way through. I think it was his second time. People just don't do that anymore."

Barbara couldn't hide her pride when the TV journalist Charlie Gibson asked her, "Have you seen anything in him that has surprised you?"

"No," she said. "But I'll tell you what I have seen. I've noticed—and his brother Jeb, the governor of Florida, told—told us this at a family dinner—that in the last five or six months, we're all sort of a tad in awe of him. Because he suddenly looks like a president. He's—he's just gotten that air and that ability. And we're very proud of him. His father and I are bursting with pride over all five of our children. But all of us in the family feel that George is doing a great job, and he's very presidential."

"The time has come to say 'enough.' Let's judge a man on what [George W.]'s done. He's been a great governor of Texas. He has done so many really important things. I think people are glad. We are tired of trashing our candidates. We are not going to get good people to run if we are going to have all these questions."

"Mothers are allowed to be proud of their sons. And it gets a little old when ten grown men run around the country not talking about what they're going to do, but knocking my precious, courageous, brilliant son. That's a mother speaking."

The journalist Karen Brown once asked Barbara: "Do you think it is fair for the media to ask your so George W. whether or not he has used cocaine?"

She replied: "I think it's fair, but his father and I never asked him that. We had no need to. He's always been a fabulous son. And I think it's fair. I'm very glad he's taken the stand he has, though, because the time has come to say 'enough.' Let's judge a man on what he's done. He's been a great governor of Texas. He's done so many really important things. And I think if you put your foot down, I think people are glad. We're tired of the sort of trashing our candidates. We're not going to get good people to run if we're going to have all of these questions."

When George W. refused to discuss whether he ever used illegal drugs, Barbara said, "Do I think he had a lot of fun at college? You betcha he did. You should work very hard at everything you do, but you also ought to have fun in life. He had a lot of fun, I imagine."

She felt strongly about how the Democrats criticized her son George W., and she shared her thoughts with the press. "We knew we were going to be shot at, but you don't like it when it's your son, because they're not true the things that are being said. And that bothers you. I honestly think that George's campaign is wonderful. He's positive; he doesn't criticize the others. He's talking about issues. So I don't like to hear them say untruths."

First Mom

After her son George W. announced his bid for the presidency, Barbara Bush was asked to help out. "I'm a little surprised to find myself back on the campaign trail." Echoing her husband's famous "no-new-taxes" pledge, she added: "I am the woman who in 1992 said, 'Read my lips. No more campaigns.'"

While campaigning for her son George W., she poked fun at herself. "It is fun to get back out here and talk about somebody I really feel so very strongly about. This is the son who says to me things like, when I pick up my fork, 'Go on, Mom, eat it today and wear it tomorrow.'"

She promised that George W. would help reform the Medicare system to "make sure you have access to prescription drugs that you need." Then she added, "If he doesn't, his mother's going to kill him."

At one point during the presidential campaign of 2000, the Democrats pointed out George W.'s intention to reinvest some of the Social Security funds into the stock market in order to make more money. Barbara Bush called this revelation a "scare tactic," and said: "George W. has your best interests at heart, no matter what you may hear from the other side. The scare tactics have absolutely no place in a presidential campaign. It's politics of fear, and it happens every four years."

At another rally not long after the preceding statement, Barbara told the crowd: "You're going to hear some outrageous things about our son in the next week. Keep this in mind: Do you think this white-haired senior citizen would let George W. Bush wreck Social Security? Of course not."

When George W. joined his mother in San Antonio at the opening of the Barbara Bush Elementary School, Barbara revealed that she was "a little nervous" during the dedication ceremony. "It's been a long time since I've been invited to a meeting with the principal and one of our sons."

Barbara was naturally aghast when she learned that George W.'s underage twin daughters were caught in an Austin bar. The twins brought their friends to Camp David in an attempt to soften the blow. "To this day George Sr. is the soft touch and I'm the enforcer," she said. "I'm the one who writes them a letter and says 'Shape up!' He writes, 'You're marvelous.'"

During the time when the media was still buzzing about the twins' arrest for underage drinking, a reporter asked Barbara whatever happened to the black Trans Am she drove in around Kennebunkport, Maine.

"I had to give it up. That car was an invitation for one of the grandchildren to get arrested. And that's all we need is for another one of them—" She stopped herself in mid-sentence.

"A lot of people ask me if George W. was a rascal when he was growing up," she said. Then she deadpanned: "Of course not—he was a perfect child." She admitted hearing some people say that her son's two teenage daughters are "Barbara's revenge on George W."

Barbara Bush

"That's not true either," she said. "Those girls are perfect."

Her spin on George W.'s own drinking problems and his having to face similar issues with his twin daughters: "He is getting back some of his own."

She said that her son George W. wouldn't have a problem with foreign policy because he had raised "two wonderful, strong-willed teenage daughters. Thanks to them, there's absolutely no doubt in my mind he will be able to negotiate with any country in the world, regardless of how difficult, complicated, or stubborn the opposition is."

When the journalist Wolf Blitzer told Barbara Bush that Senator John McCain said that George W. was the "establishment candidate" after being endorsed by countless congressmen and governors, she said: "That really makes me laugh. Who's been in Washington eighteen years? And who's been out in the country working and then being governor? I think the action today, Wolf, is in the states, in the governors. They're making the difference. George knows what the people want. And I think for us—"us" meaning George's campaign—to let the McCain campaign—where he's been there eighteen years—put the establishment on George is absolutely ridiculous. And I don't blame him for trying, but I think that's ridiculous."

While standing before a crowd of senior citizens, she tried her best not to break a promise not to mention the candidate Al Gore by name. "Please notice that I have been very good about not mentioning the opponent's name. Although I'm dying to point out that he had very bad manners during the debate and a huge tendency to exaggerate. I promised George, my husband, this morning, that I'm not going to do it—wouldn't be prudent—and that I would behave myself."

"I've only given [George W.] one piece of advice, which is you're natural, and be natural. I mean, that's what people like. And I've resisted sending that every day."

Barbara Bush

She claimed that her son learned a great deal from Texas politics: "If you want to get things done in government, you better learn to compromise."

Upon endorsing their son as the next president of the United States, Barbara shared her husband's pride. "It's overwhelming for a mother to say those words," she said. "Both his father and I realize our brains are in tune with our hearts. George W. is truly the right person to lead this country into the next century."

After seeing that *Saturday Night Live* had poked fun at her son George W. during his presidential campaign by trying to use Scrabble tiles to make the word "dignitude," Barbara said, "When people say he isn't smart…I just go ballistic."

Barbara didn't like to follow her son George W.'s campaign as closely as her husband did. "My stomach is churning and I don't take criticism of my children very well. So you can imagine how much I like turning on the news all the time."

First Mom

"I'm glib and I think sometimes George is, which is to his detriment sometimes," she said. "When his father had a sense of humor and told a joke, the press always wrote it up as though he was dead serious. George should have learned a lesson from that. You can't go around taking yourself so darned seriously all the time, but I think he's got to be careful [about being too flippant]."

In a poll on which candidate—George W. or Al Gore—was better-looking, she said, "I thought that was the dumbest poll—until I saw who won."

When asked about George W.'s positions on the environment and health care in New Hampshire, she said, "He has position papers on those, and you can look at the campaign Internet site. I felt free speaking for my husband. I'm not as confident speaking for my son. I don't dare speak for him. He'd kill me."

Diana Olick had a sit-down with Barbara about the mudslinging during the presidential race of 2000.

DIANA OLICK: Well, when you hear it, I imagine with

your husband, it's got to be a bit different than when they're going after your child.

BARBARA BUSH: Much worse, much worse.

DIANA: How do you handle that?

BARBARA: My fifty-four-year-old child. I hate it. And his father doesn't like it very much either.

It is clear that even though Barbara Bush often protested that she's not "an elected official," she really knows her money, as revealed in her conversation with the TV journalist Wolf Blitzer during the presidential race of 2000.

WOLF BLITZER: We catch you in the middle of this campaign, and you're obviously campaigning for your son. Why do you think Governor Bush would be a better president than Senator McCain?

BARBARA BUSH: Well, I think there are a lot of reasons, Wolf. Number one, I think he's been in the private sector, which is very important. He not only built a business, but he also built a ballpark and managed the team. And then he was governor. And I think—and I think most Republicans think—that government on the local level is better than government on the national level. Eighteen years in Congress is fine, and I think John McCain's a courageous, wonderful citizen. But having said that, why, you know, thirty-five–thirty-seven Republican governors have endorsed George W., and 175 Republican congressmen have endorsed him. I think that's really unprecedented; 171,000 Americans have sent George W. money, averaging $340...

Barbara admitted amazement at the millions of dollars that George W.'s popularity had helped raise during his presidential race. "We'd have given up several of the grandchildren for that kind of money" in the 1992 campaign. She paused before adding, "I'm kidding, of course."

At one point during her son's presidential campaign, Barbara told audiences that her son had "increased the pay of each and every teacher $8,500." But the next day the figure swelled to $18,000, which quickly dropped to $8,000 once she focused on her script. "I don't want to lie to you," she said as she realized her error, then added, "I'm not above it, though."

While campaigning for her son George W., she told an appreciative crowd: "I just want to remind you that every vote counts. Vote early, and then vote often. That's what we do in Texas."

Early on in George W.'s campaign for the presidency, she told Republican supporters at a fund-raiser: "It's going to be a terrible, tough, mean, ugly year. That's a mother speaking."

"George got a lot from me, but one thing he didn't get from me was nerves. He's calm. I think he's got a much better attitude than I have. His attitude is, 'Look, I'm going to try my very hardest, I'm going to do my very best, and if it works, I'm going to be the best president I can, and if not, Laura and I have a great life out there.'"

When she heard Al Gore's initial concession to George W. in the historic November 7, 2000 election, she said, "I was the mother of a president for thirty minutes, and I loved it."

When the country was in suspense over the out-come of the historic election—did Gore or Bush win? —Barbara told a reporter: "We sort of feel like the VCR is stuck on pause. We are nervous, but we're really doing just fine, taking each day and each court ruling as it comes."

"I've often wondered what would have happened if George W. had walked out, said to his people, look, you've been standing there in the rain forever, it's three in the morning, Al Gore has very graciously called me. I'm going to come out in the morning, and

Barbara Bush

we'll discuss the future plans. I am the president-
elect. What would have happened?"

After her son George W. was finally declared victor
in the presidential race, she said, "You be nice to
him now. I want to start reading magazines and
papers again....I'm going to start reading again. But
I'm giving you fair warning."

"As an American, I could not be happier to have
this decent, wise man in the White House."

"I am probably the only mom in America who
knows exactly what her son is doing and where he is
doing it."

"I'm now thinking the whole pretzel incident may
have been his [George W.'s] heaven-sent punishment
for making fun of my cooking," Barbara Bush joked
about Forty-three having fainted the previous month
after choking on a pretzel. "It was the president
choking on his words."

First Mom

Referring to her husband and his place in the presidential order, Barbara said, "Obviously, both Forty-one and I are very, very proud of our president. Sometimes, when George and I watch our son, such as last week when he spoke to the nation about Iraq, we truly are in awe...." She wondered, "Can this be that same miserable little kid that I used to threaten with death?"

When Diane Sawyer asked whether it was tempting to "rush" back to the White House to help their son George W. during Operation Iraqi Freedom, Barbara said, "We have e-mail and telephones. No, it isn't tempting."

"Quite frankly it's a relief for me to be out of the house and away from the television set," she said during a speech when her son George W. was involved with Operation Iraqi Freedom.

"[George and I] didn't even know he wanted to get married until he showed up at the door with this beautiful creature, Laura, and announced that she

was going to be his wife."

During the presidential race of 2000, Barbara compared her daughter-in-law to Hillary Clinton.

"She's quiet. She's strong. She's bright. She's funny. She'd be a wonderful First Lady [standing] at his side, supporting him in every way."

She also felt that Laura Bush had shared "a great philosophy in life—you can either like it or not, so you might as well like it."

"Mothers are allowed to be proud of their sons.

First Mom

And it gets a little old when ten grown men run around the country not talking about what they're going to do, but knocking my precious, courageous, brilliant son. That's a mother speaking."

On her daughter-in-law, Laura Bush, she said: "Laura's quiet, but she accomplishes a lot with that quietness."

"George W. is doing just fine without his mother trying to help."

"I hated it when anyone criticized my brilliant husband, and I'm furious when they criticize my son."

"Now that I'm the mother of a president, I can say almost anything I want and get away with it."

Barbara Bush

Millie and Ranger

Barbara made an appearance on Larry King's show to plug her bestselling book *Millie's Book: As Dictated to Barbara Bush.*

LARRY KING: Ladies and gentlemen, the First Lady of the United States, who brought me a gift tonight—and this is a treasure—when we were at the White House two weeks ago—they're writing a second book with Millie, right? Second book is coming, and they took pictures.

BARBARA BUSH: Millie's writing it....

LARRY: Millie's writing a book. And this is the picture—let me hold this—this is me interviewing Millie.

BARBARA: He wants to be on the cover, but I don't think so.

LARRY: Look at that. What is Millie saying here? What is my question—what is Millie saying?

BARBARA: She's saying, "I'm not going to tell you that, Larry."

She joked that Millie was far more popular than she during her Second Lady years. "I mean, Millie made the front page of the paper when I casually said she was getting married."

During a discussion of *Millie's Book*, it was pointed out that Barbara herself—as "Millie's mother"—was extremely popular as well. She said, "That might be because she's married to the president. Funny, nobody was knocking themselves down to get to her before."

Barbara said that Millie liked to take showers. "Millie, of course, does not take them alone because she's too short to reach up. But someone, a very high public official elected to office, takes a shower with Millie every week or so." A few moments later she had second thoughts about what she'd shared. "I hope that same public official won't be sore at me."

Barbara Bush

Once, while entertaining the Australian prime minister Robert J. L. Hawke, Barbara found Millie dropping a tennis ball from her mouth in front of Barbara. She quipped, "I gave her a clean one in honor of the prime minister."

On meeting Ranger, the son of their dog Millie, she said that George "came in the other day with some stranger and he said, 'Come on in, I want you to meet the love of my life—here, Ranger.'"

On the idea of doing a book with Ranger, she said, "I'm thinking about helping Ranger do *Ranger's Revenge*, but we're not there yet. He's still a baby. He does love the president, though. The president loves him."

Barbara Bush

Post-White House Life

S he compared the dramatic flavor of her life with
George on their last night in the White House:
"On January twentieth [1993] we woke up and we
had a household staff of ninety-three. The very next
morning we woke up and it was George, me, and two
dogs—and that's not all that bad."

"I sometimes find retirement so exhausting that I
think I'll get a job."

After leaving the White House, Barbara confessed
that her days with George have been nothing short
of wonderful: "We've discovered there is great joy in
growing older and being unemployed."

"I don't miss one darn thing [about living in
the White House]. I loved being the wife of the

president, but anyone who wants something that's gone, or that they can't have, is stupid. I hate it when people whine about something they can't have. Life doesn't end after the presidency. People still come to your charity events; they're still kind and nice on the street. If I have any complaint about being the wife of the former president, it's that I can't go mingling in the stores and be a private person."

Barbara shared her thoughts on her post–White House years with Larry King on his TV program *Larry King Live.*

LARRY KING: When you get back to private life—what's been the toughest part—the toughest adjustment?

BARBARA BUSH: This is honestly true, and it sounds a little bit selfish, but it never occurred to me that I could never walk down the street again. I always loved walking in Kennebunkport down the ocean drive to downtown and back. It was good exercise and I loved doing it. People drive off the road now, they ask you—

LARRY: You go shopping with George though, right, you go to—

BARBARA: Well, we race; he stops and signs autographs and I race through and shop. But–

LARRY: But there's no normal life?

BARBARA: He's much more generous than I am.

LARRY: Do you miss–you're driving sedans with…

BARBARA: No, no, I drive.

LARRY: You drive? Does the Supreme Court–is the Secret Service in front of you and behind you?

BARBARA: No, I just drive.

LARRY: Barbara!

BARBARA: Watch out for me on the road! Watch out, she's on the road!

About her activities after leaving the White House, she admitted, "I had to give up tennis because it's hard on my hips. So I'm struggling on the golf course. I've played all over the country when George has been speaking at conferences. I still read all the time and do needlepoint–and my computer is my best friend. The children will tell you I've overly organized. I have no paper. Everything's in the computer. I do recipes, addresses, my calendar, my diary, and all my speeches on it."

Barbara sometimes thanked her audiences for showing up whenever she and her husband appeared, as she and George were only "a couple of unemployed senior citizens."

When Barbara saw the students protesting her five-figure speaking fee with signs like PROFITS OVER PEOPLE at Kent State University, she told the $10-a-ticket audience: "When I was just Mrs. Now-out-of-office-George-Bush, no one even showed up to yell at me. It's sort of flattering to be yelled at again."

"A perfectly strange, attractive woman came over, put her face in mine, and said, 'Aren't you somebody? I know I know you.' She never took a breath and continued, 'Are you a teacher? Have you waited on me in a store? Didn't you help me at Sears?' I never had a chance to say a word but just kept nodding. She left as quickly as she arrived, muttering as she went: 'I thought she was somebody.'"

When she fielded questions from the audience after a speech, Barbara Bush paused while discussing her four children who are not in public office. "Imagine," she said as if the idea had just struck her, "getting paid to talk about your children!"

She reflected on her just-published book, *Barbara Bush: A Memoir,* on Larry King's TV program. "It turned out to be absolutely the best thing that could have happened to me. I loved writing it...because I always knew that I was lucky and that life had been good to me; but I really remembered again how really good it had been."

On his TV program *Larry King Live,* the interviewer Larry King quizzed Barbara Bush on why she wrote *Barbara Bush: A Memoir.*

BARBARA BUSH: Well, because I—I really didn't plan to write a book, but three publishers came to me at the White House after George lost and said, "We would like to publish your book." I said, "Well, I don't have a book." And they said, "It's a well-known fact that you have kept diaries." And then they offered me a sum I couldn't say no to, I'm going to tell you the honest truth.

LARRY KING: That kind of offer?

BARBARA: That kind of offer; it was very nice.

When asked why she, a very private person, would write an autobiography, she said, "Because my husband couldn't keep a job."

During their winter months in Houston during the post–White House years, she went to bed early with her husband. "We've never been night owls. We're always the first to leave a dinner party."

At the lavish bash thrown at the Grand Ole Opry in honor of Barbara and George's fiftieth wedding anniversary, she admitted, "One [of my children] said to me, 'Mother, we just can't afford all these events you're having every year.' But I just love my life."

On her new home in Houston, she said, "We built this house, and I love it. It has only three bedrooms, but there's an elevator that goes up three floors. It has beautiful light. The Secret Service agents are like family now, but they don't live in our house. The best thing is we live next door to best friends."

"I'm seventy-four now. My husband's out of office—if I don't like your question, I'm not going to answer it."

After eight years away from the White House, she shared her future plans about her son if he won. "I can't walk out of the house in Kennebunkport without someone coming up to me. But when George is president, I can tell you, I don't plan to be in Washington much."

Whenever George and she eat alone these days, they eat simply. "I think we're every doctor's horror. Last week we had an evening home alone and we had cheese omelets, bacon, and toast. Just the wrong things, of course."

Barbara has this to say about their post–White House years: "It's been different. I started driving again. I started cooking again. My driving's better than my cooking. George has discovered Sam's Club."

First Mom

By January 16, 2003, former First Lady Barbara Bush had delivered ten speeches in ten different cities in the new year alone. "And George and I are supposedly unemployed and retired!"

She admitted to being addicted to the TV show *Survivor*: "George and I know what it's like to be voted off the island."

September 11, 2001

After the September 11 attacks, she reminded her fans that "we must fight evil not only with force, but also with generosity, love, and friendship."

"The days after 9/11 were confusing for us all. How could people accept our hospitality for years, be educated at our universities, and live among us while planning to kill us?"

"Since 9/11...it's more important than ever to remind ourselves that tolerance is one of the most important of human qualities. We need to learn to appreciate and celebrate the differences in people, rather than fear or resent them. I agree with the teacher who said we can all learn from crayons: Some are sharp, some are pretty, some are dull, some have weird names, and all are different colors...but they all have to learn to live in the same box."

Barbara expressed hope that after the September 11 attacks, Americans would pray for "world peace. And when people say to me—and they say it through airports, through railroad stations, through everything—'We're praying for your son,' I know they're saying, 'We're praying for the world.' That's what they're praying for. I know that...I see no animosity, I see great affection. I'm not saying everybody's for him, but I see people know he's doing his best. And he's decent and honest and kind, and he doesn't think he knows everything. He's got a great team, and that's very important. But when it gets down to it, it's the president [who has to make the decisions]."

Reflecting on her son's restraint in not responding with an immediate attack after the events of September 11, she confessed to *Newsweek:* "I'm not sure I'd have been that good."

"You know the way to really help our country,

Barbara Bush

truthfully? I spoke at a big lunch today, and [the organizers] said, 'We were so afraid you wouldn't come if something had happened.' I said, 'I'd have been here much quicker if something had happened.' Because that's what we have to do. You can't let them win! We've got to work for our country, and the way people like me can do it is to go and encourage people and help them raise a lot of money for their charities."

"You could say tonight is all about heroes," she said to a group of supporters. In the time since the September 11 attacks, "we have been reminded over and over again why we're so darn proud to be American."

Barbara Bush

Wisdom and Advice

"I'm going to share some of the things I've learned in seventy-six years of life, fifty-seven years of marriage, six children, fourteen grandchildren, five wars, three dress sizes, two governors, two parachute jumps and, now two presidents."

"When something terrible happens, unless you make it something good come out of it, then a whole life is wasted."

"If I could give people one piece of advice, it would be, 'Never go up to someone and say that you didn't vote for her husband.'"

"[George] gave me some very important advice... 'Be nice to your kids. They'll choose your nursing home.'"

"Home is not a house or a city, but wherever you and your family are. Even the White House, as big and imposing as it was, felt like home because it was where we lived and where our children and grandchildren came to visit."

"The most important job any of us will ever have is parenting," said Barbara. "The home is our children's first school, and we are their first teachers."

"Persist in teaching your children! They are impressionable. They listen to us. If children don't listen to us, they will listen to TV, video games, and their friends—and they will get the wrong messages."

"Turn off the television and talk to your children, then listen to what they are telling you. Leave the unwashed dishes and dirty laundry for later. Your children are only young once, so cherish the early years and set a good example for them to follow."

"You have to love your children unselfishly. That is hard. But it is the only way."

Barbara Bush

"Don't ever lend your car to someone you gave birth to or they gave birth to."

"I believe in passages, times in your life. I think there was a time in my life where I really nested and was a mother. And then, I mean, I went to China and really delved deeply into it, into the history. I really think it's good for you to get a new subject about every ten years. Unless you have a burning desire to be a doctor or a president of a bank, probably it's a good thing to shift jobs, meet new people, take on new projects."

"Some people give time, some money, some their skills and connections, some literally give their life's blood. But everyone has something to give."

"I know that many of you give to charities," she said. "Sometimes that's not enough. It's important to find a cause that you can feel passionate about."

"Work conquers all," Barbara once said, "but that isn't enough. Have a career and have a life," she said, "but be sure you never confuse the two."

First Mom

"Cherish your human connections: your relationships with friends and family."

"At the end of your life, you will never regret not having passed one more test, winning one more verdict, or not closing one more deal. You will regret

Barbara Bush

time not spent with a husband, a child, a friend, or a parent."

"Get involved in some of the big ideas of your time."

First Mom

"Protocol is not there to dictate you. It's there to help you. You have to have the courage to do it your way."

"Never give up!" she advised. "I have learned the longer we persevere, the greater our blessings become."

"Giving frees us from the familiar territory of our own needs by opening our mind to the unexplained worlds occupied by the needs of others."

"The winner of the hoop race will be the first to realize her dream, not society's dream, her own personal dream."

"Never lose sight of the fact that the most important yardstick of your success will be how you treat other people—your family, friends, and coworkers, and even strangers you meet along the way."

"You just don't luck into things as much as you'd like to think you do. You build step by step, whether

"For heaven's sake, enjoy life! Don't cry over things that were or things that aren't."

"Life is a gift, and we must not waste it."

"Having a big heart has nothing to do with your bank account; everyone has something to give!"

"When you come to a roadblock, take a detour."

"Only the actions of the just smell sweet and blossom in the dust."

"A single act of kindness can make us citizens, not spectators."

"If human beings are perceived as potentials rather than problems, as possessing strengths instead of weaknesses, as unlimited rather than dull and unresponsive, then they thrive and grow to their capabilities."

First Mom

"People say to me all the time, 'Oh, Barbara, times have changed.' Well, right is right and wrong is wrong, and we know the difference. They haven't changed. We need to take responsibility—for ourselves, for our children, and for our neighbors."

"Study hard. There's no such thing as knowing too much. After all, you all want to grow up and be on *Who Wants to Be a Millionaire*, don't you?"

"Learning is what life is all about."

"Happiness is something you decide on ahead of time," she said. "Deposit a lot of happiness in the bank account of memories—starting right now."

"Families in America today are struggling, and too often we blame government because of laws that have or have not been passed instead of accepting the blame ourselves. We expect teachers to be church leaders, psychiatrists. The responsibility for strong families rests with you and me."

Barbara Bush

"To us, family means putting your arms around each other and being there."

First Mom

"You have to adore someone who adores you."

"What happens in the White House doesn't matter half as much as what happens in your house."

"People are like crayons," she said. "Some are sharp, some are dull, some have odd names, and they're all different colors, but they have to learn to live together in the same box."

"If you can remain calm, then obviously you don't know what's going on," she said. "And you can't hide a piece of broccoli in a glass of milk; now, that would be very funny if I was talking about a grandchild."

Barbara's Ten Life Lessons:
1. Learn not to take life too seriously or things too personally.
2. Never ask someone over seventy years of age how he or she feels.
3. When your grandchildren come to visit, be careful of criticizing their clothes.
4. Remind yourself of what's really important in

Barbara Bush

life and what's not. 207

5. You usually get out of life what you put into it.

6. Don't forget to have fun.

7. Take an active part in your community.

8. Don't forget to spend quality time with your children.

9. Don't forget to read to your children and grandchildren.

10. Don't be afraid of adversity in your personal life.

First Mom

Barbara Bush

Barbara Bush's

Wellesley Commencement Speech

Friday, June 1, 1990

I am thrilled to be with you today, and very excited, as I know you must all be, that Mrs. Gorbachev could join us. This is an exciting time in Washington, D.C. But I am so glad to be here. I knew coming to Wellesley would be fun, but I never dreamed it would be this much fun.

More than ten years ago, when I was invited here to talk about our experiences in the People's Republic of China, I was struck by both the natural beauty of your campus and the spirit of this place. Wellesley, you see, is not just a place, but an idea...an experiment in excellence in which diversity is not just tolerated but is embraced.

The essence of this spirit was captured in a moving speech about tolerance given last year by the student body president of one of your sister colleges. She related the story by Robert Fulghum about a young pastor who, finding himself in charge of some very energetic children, hits upon a game called Giants, Wizards, and Dwarfs.

"You have to decide now," the pastor instructed the children, "which you are—a giant, a wizard, or a dwarf."

At that, a small girl tugging at his pants leg asked, "But where do the mermaids stand?"

The pastor told her there are no mermaids, and she said, "Oh, yes, there are. I am a mermaid."

Now, this little girl knew what she was, and she was not about to give up on either her identity or the game. She intended to take her place wherever mermaids fit into the scheme of things. Where do the mermaids stand...all those who are different, those who do not fit the boxes and pigeonholes? "Answer that question," wrote Fulghum, "and you can build a school, a nation, or a whole world."

As that very wise young woman said, "Diversity, like anything worth having, requires effort." Effort to learn about and respect difference, to be compassionate with one another, to cherish our own identity, and to accept unconditionally the same in others.

Barbara Bush

You should all be very proud that this is the Wellesley
spirit. Now, I know your first choice today was Alice
Walker, known for [her Pulitzer Prize-winning novel]
The Color Purple. And guess how I know?

Instead, you got me—known for the color of my
hair! Alice Walker's book has a special resonance
here. At Wellesley, each class is known by a special
color; for four years the class of '90 has worn the
color purple. Today you meet on Severence Green
to say good-bye to all of that...to begin a new and
very personal journey...to search for your own true
colors.

In the world that awaits you beyond the shores of
Lake Waban, no one can say what your true colors
will be. But this I do know: You have a first-class
education from a first-class school. And so you need
not, probably cannot, live a "paint-by-numbers" life.
Decisions are not irrevocable. Choices do come back.
As you set off from Wellesley, I hope that many of
you will consider making three very special choices.

The first is to believe in something larger than
yourself....to get involved in some of the big ideas
of your time. I chose literacy because I honestly

First Mom

believe that if more people could read, write, and comprehend, we would be that much closer to solving so many of the problems plaguing our society.

Early on I made another choice which I hope you will make as well. Whether you are talking about education, career, or service, you are talking about life...and life must have joy. It's supposed to be fun! One of the reasons I made the most important decision of my life...to marry George Bush...is because he made me laugh. It's true, sometimes we've laughed through our tears...but that shared laughter has been one of our strongest bonds. Find the joy in life, because as Ferris Bueller said on his day off: "Life moves pretty fast. Ya don't stop and look around once in a while, ya gonna miss it!"

I won't tell George that you applauded Ferris more than you applauded him!

The third choice that must not be missed is to cherish your human connections: your relationships with friends and family. For several years you've had impressed upon you the importance to your career of dedication and hard work. This is true, but as important as your obligations as a doctor, lawyer, or business leader will be, you are a human being first, and those human connections—with spouses, with children, with friends—are the most important investments you will ever make.

At the end of your life you will never regret not having passed one more test, not winning one more verdict, or not closing one more deal. You will regret time not spent with a husband, a friend, a child, or a parent.

We are in a transitional period right now...fascinating and exhilarating times...learning to adjust to the changes and the choices we...men and women... are facing.

As an example, I remember what a friend said on hearing her husband complain to his buddies that he had to baby-sit. Quickly setting him straight...my friend told her husband that when it's your own kids . . . it's not called "baby-sitting"!

Maybe we should adjust faster, maybe slower. But whatever the era...whatever the times, one thing will never change: Fathers and mothers, if you have children...they must come first. You must read to your children, you must hug your children, you must love your children.

Your success as a family...our success as a society... depends not on what happens at the White House but on what happens inside your house.

For over fifty years, it was said that the winner of Wellesley's annual hoop race would be the first to get married. Now they say the winner will be the first to become a CEO. Both of those stereotypes show too little tolerance for those who want to know where the mermaids stand. So I want to offer you today a new legend: The winner of the hoop race will be the first to realize her dream...not society's dream...her own personal dream. Who knows? Somewhere out in this audience may even be someone who will one day follow in my footsteps, and preside over the White House as the president's spouse. I wish him well!

The controversy ends here. But our conversation is only beginning. And a worthwhile conversation it has been. So as you leave Wellesley today, take with you deep thanks for the courtesy and the honor you have shared with Mrs. Gorbachev and me. Thank you. God bless you. And may your future be worthy of your dreams.

Barbara Bush